D0382452

# Christian Mysticism

THE MYSTIC LIBRARY

# Christian Mysticism

Manuela Dunn Mascetti

*Introduction by Peter Roche de Coppens, Ph. D.*

HYPERION

NEW YORK

Copyright © 1998 Manuela Dunn Mascetti
Introduction © 1998 Peter Roche de Coppens, Ph. D.


All rights reserved. No part of this book may be used or reproduced in
any manner whatsoever without the written permission of the Publisher.

For information address:
Hyperion, 114 Fifth Avenue, New York, NY 10011



Designed by MoonRunner Design, Dorset, UK
Image selection by MoonRunner Design, Dorset, UK




Printed in the United States of America


ISBN 0-7868-6330-7



FIRST EDITION
10 9 8 7 6 5 4 3 2 1

*Christus Pantokrator.*
Mosaic in the
chapel of the
Chora Monastery
in Constantinople,
14th c.

*Jesus said, "If you bring forth what is within you, what you bring*

*forth will save you. If you do not bring forth what is within you,*

*what you do not bring forth will destroy you."*

— J. M. Robinson, *The Nag Hammadi Library*

# Contents

# PART III. SEEKING THE TRUTH

# *Introduction*

*HE* M*YSTIC* L*IBRARY* OF WHICH THIS WORK, *Christian Mysticism*, is the second volume could not be more timely and important. Through both words and illustrations and in its descriptive and allegorical style it answers one of the deepest longings of humanity and is most appropriate for the present historical period in which we are all spectators and actors, for it goes to the very heart of the great challenge brought about by the end of our century and of the second millennium.

Today, we are all living at a historical time and cultural juncture where a massive transition and transformation is taking place, both at the quantitative and at the qualitative level. This involves, among many other things, a massive expansion and heightening of human consciousness, which is bound to bring about major psychosocial, cultural, and spiritual transformations. Practically all social institutions worldwide—from education to health care and from politics to religion and involving all aspects of our lives, both individual and collective—are presently in a state of crisis, which implies real and great dangers and just as real and great opportunities.

At this time, the passage from the "horizontal" (external, physical) dimension to the "vertical" (internal, psycho-spiritual) dimension is required of all of us, whether we know it and like it or not, and mysticism holds the key to that fundamental passage. This is the reason why some of the greatest thinkers of our times have declared:

"The 21$^{st}$ century will be spiritual. . . or will not be" (André Malraux)

"Below (in lower states of consciousness) there no more solutions, while above (in higher states of consciousness) there are no problems" (Roberto Assagioli)

"The greatest challenge and newest frontier of the future can no longer be the physical one, they must become the spiritual one" (Arnold Toynbee)

These incisive and perceptive statements actually repeat and highlight, in different words, Jesus' long-ago statement: "What shall profit a man if he gains the whole world but loses his soul?", which I translate to mean "What will happen to me if I gain everything—money, power, position—in the outer world but can no longer perceive meaning, purpose, beauty, and value in what I am, in what I have, and in what I live?"

Certain events in my own life led me towards religion as a possible source for such an answer. Today, I am convinced that religion does, in fact, hold the solutions to the most important problems of human life and to suffering in particular. I am not speaking of the "exoteric" (official, external) side of religion, but rather its "esoteric" (internal and personally lived) aspects.

What I call the "esoteric" side of religion is what is generally known as the "mystical side," or mysticism, which is based upon the direct personal observation and experience of the deeper aspects of Reality with which one has united or become "at one" with. Hence, it is in the domain of mystical spirituality and direct personal experience of the deeper aspects and laws of the universe and of oneself where one must look for such answers and for the real key to human life. Hence, the vital and timely importance of this series and of its present volume, *Christian Mysticism*.

What is mysticism, or the esoteric side of religion? Let us briefly turn to Evelyn Underhill, a world-recognized expert in this area for the first half of this century:

> To be a mystic is to simply participate here and now in the real and eternal
> life: in the fullest, deepest sense which is possible to man. It is to share, as a
> free and conscious agent—not as a servant, but as a son—in the joyous tra-
> vail of the Universe: its mighty onward sweep through pain and glory to its
> home in God. This gift of "sonship," this power of free cooperation in the
> world-process, is man's greatest honor . . . . The mystic knows that destiny.
> It is laid bare to his lucid vision, as plain to him as our puzzling world of
> form and color is to the normal sight. He is the "hidden child" of the eternal
> order, an initiate of the secret plan . . . . He is the pioneer of Life in its age-long

*journey to the One: and shows us, in his attainment, the meaning and value of that life . . . . According to the measure of their strength and of their passions, these true lovers of the Absolute have conformed here and now to the utmost tests of divine sonship, the final demands of life. They have not shrunk from the sufferings of the cross. They have faced the darkness of the tomb. Beauty and agony alike have called them: alike have awakened a heroic response. But for them the winter is over: the time of the singing of birds is come. But from the deeps of the dewy garden, Life—new, unquenchable and ever lovely—comes to meet them with the dawn.*

And

*Far from being academic or unreal [mysticism], I think is vital for the deeper understanding of the history of humanity. It shows us, upon high levels, the psychological process to which every self desires to rise to the perception of Reality and must submit to the formula under which man's spiritual consciousness, be it strong or weak, must necessarily unfold. In the greatest mystics we see the highest and widest development of that consciousness to which the human race has yet attained . . . . But the germ of that same transcendent life, the spring of the amazing energy which enables the great mystic to rise to freedom and dominate his world, is latent in all of us: an integral part of our humanity. Where the mystic has a genius for the Absolute, we have each a little buried talent, some greater some less: and the growth of this talent, this spark of soul, once we permit its emergence, will conform in little, and according to its measure, to those inexorable conditions of transcendence which we found govern the Mystic Way. . . .*

Finally, she concludes that:

*The most highly developed branches of the human family have in common one peculiar characteristic. They tend to produce—sporadically, it is true, and usually in the teeth of adverse external circumstances—a curious and definite type of personality: a type which refuses to be satisfied with that which other men call experience, and is inclined, in the words of its enemies,*

*to "deny the world in order that it may find reality." We meet these persons in the east and the west; in ancient medieval and modern worlds. Their passion appears to be the prosecution of a certain spiritual and intangible quest: the finding of a "way out" or a "way back" to some desirable state in which, alone, they can satisfy their craving for absolute truth. This quest, for them, has constituted the whole meaning of life: they have made, without effort, sacrifices which have appeared enormous to other men: and it is an indirect testimony to its objective reality, that whatever the place or period in which they have arisen, their aims, doctrines, and meth-*

Oil on wood painting, Exeter Cathedral.

*ods have been substantially the same. Their experience, therefore, forms a body of evidence, curiously self-consistent and often mutually explanatory, which must be taken into account before we can add up the sum of the energies and potentialities of the human spirit; or reasonably speculate on its relations to the unknown world which lies outside the boundaries of sense.*

To become a mystic, to enter the esoteric side of religion, one must undergo a general and progressive training leading to the purification and consecration of one's being and to the transformation and expansion of one's consciousness. This is best achieved by proceeding gradually from the "exoteric" to the "esoteric" aspect of religion. To fly, a bird (which has long been the symbol of human consciousness, or the soul in many cultures and traditions) needs two wings. One wing represents tradition, the long and time-tested experience of many men and women under appropriate supervision, the other direct personal vision and experience in higher states of consciousness. The great world religions have always provided an authentic tradition if, at times, the "direct and personal vision and experience" remained hidden and latent because external circumstances were quite dangerous for this type of adventure or because of lack of genuine "spiritual fathers and mothers," proper guides who can lead the serious aspirant on the path to spiritual illumination in a safe and effective way.

*Maria with the Child, accompanied by the Holy Agnes, Barbara, and Dorothea,* from the central panel of the Ortenberger Altarpiece, c. 1425 C.E.

This work, *Christian Mysticism,* provides an excellent source and springboard for both those who are interested in better understanding Christianity, in its doctrinal foundation and historical unfolding, and for those who aspire to become Christian mystics and realize the heart and core of this religion in their own beings and lives. In a very simple and straightforward way, and especially avoiding the many philosophical and theological controversies that have always plagued religion and been most counterproductive, the author has succeeded in providing a truly "global view" of Christianity in a language, images and metaphors, that are accessible to all, believers and unbelievers, beginners and more experienced persons.

In a few pages, complemented by splendid illustrations, the author has provided the gist of the Christian legend and mysteries, of the life and teachings of Jesus of Nazareth, and of the history of primitive Christianity and its splintering into the Eastern and Western branches. She also offers a bird's-eye view into the Eastern and Western mystical tradition by making available direct quotes and a synthesis of the teachings of some of the greatest Christian mystics. Finally, she succeeded in illustrating and suggesting basic spiritual exercises, such as prayer, meditation, and the rosary, as well as providing a contemporary list of schools and centers where the interested reader can continue and deepen the quest initiated by reading this book.

Obviously, mysticism, spirituality, and the esoteric aspect of religion cannot be adequately described and understood in intellectual terms. They must, necessarily, be a personally lived experience which only the spiritual Self, the Christ-within, can provide in His own time, when a person is ready. But one must begin somewhere and have tools with which to do the inner work. This book provides such opportunity and tools for the serious candidate.

Life on earth is a great and very complex adventure comprised of many different "adventures." The greatest and the most important of these is unquestionably the *spiritual adventure*, because it is the only quest and way that leads one to the very heart and core of Reality and of oneself. Today, with all the incredible transformations and developments that are taking place on earth and in the human psyche, the spiritual adventure has become more important than ever as it may well be our last "living Source" of authentic meaning and comprehension (for the mind), motivation and appreciation (for the heart), and energy and strength (for the will). This work offers a very simple yet profound and authentic "support," or "map" for understanding and living the Western spiritual tradition. As such it is highly recommended to both lay and professional persons, believers and unbelievers, and beginning or advanced students of the magnificent adventure of life. This series and work in particular provide the theoretical framework and the tools, but you—each one of you— must live and personalize this adventure which, of all, is the greatest and most important!

—Peter Roche de Coppens, October 1997

Quotes are from Evelyn Underhill. *Mysticism*. New York: E. P. Dutton & Co., 1919. (1: pages 534–539, 2: pages 531–532, 3: pages 3–4)

# PART I

## THE WORLD TEACHER

# Chapter One

## The Christian Legend

For to us a child is born,
to us a son is given,
and the government shall be upon his shoulder,
and his name shall be called
"Wonderful Counsellor, Mighty God,
Everlasting Father, Prince of Peace."
Of the increase of his government and of his peace
there will be no end,
upon the throne of David, and over his kingdom,
to establish it, and to uphold it
with Justice and with righteousness,
from this time forth and for ever more.
The zeal of the Lord of hosts will do this.
—Isaiah 9:6–7

I saw in the night visions,
and behold, with the clouds of heaven
there came one like a son of man.
He came to the Ancient of Days
and was presented before him.
And to him was given dominion
and glory and kingdom,
that all peoples, nations, and languages
should serve him.
His dominion is an everlasting dominion,
which shall not pass away.
And his kingdom one
that shall not be destroyed.
—Daniel 7:13–14

*Heavenly Jerusalem,* illumination on parchment, from *Augustinus, De Cvitate Dei.*

T HE Scriptures of Israel long foretold of a coming leader who would consummate the fulfillment of the divine will on earth. He would manifest the righteousness and compassion of God, bring about the final defeat of evil, and establish the Kingdom of Heaven on earth. The Hebrew title for this leader was *Messiah*—Christ in Greek—meaning "the anointed one," the person who would be specially chosen by God for this mission and empowered to accomplish it. Furthermore it was commonly believed by Jews that the Messiah would be born to the royal dynasty of King David, the great leader of the past who in Jewish tradition became the ideal king, the founder of an enduring dynasty around whose figure and reign clustered the messianic expectations of the people of Israel.

King David was the second of the Israelite kings, reigning after Saul from approximately 1000 to 962 B.C.E., establishing a united kingdom over all Israel with Jerusalem, the city he had conquered in his youth from the Jebusites as its capital. Under King David's rule Jerusalem became the holy city of the new kingdom of the Hebrew tribes, the seat of political and divine power at the heart of the Promised Land. In gratefulness to God, who had continuously guided and supported him in his rise to supremacy, David built a temple in Jerusalem when he became king and placed the ark of the Covenant—the supreme and central object of worship for the Hebrew tribes—in the Holy of Holies, a chamber in the Temple that could only be entered by high priests. With this gesture he linked his reign to God and to the premonarchic experience of Israel. According to tradition, the ark had traveled with Israel through the wilderness from Mount Sinai, where it was first built to contain the stone tablets of the law that bore the commandments God had chiseled onto them, and it was believed that the ark led the way for the tribes toward the founding of the Promised Land. It was a rectangular wooden box, originally without a cover, that established and located the presence of Yahweh with the people of Israel. The ark was carried into battle to demonstrate that Yahweh fought for Israel, and it was carried in the wilderness to show that God traveled with his people—it was a sign and even the embodiment of Yahweh's presence. By building the Temple and bringing the ark to Jerusalem, King David became the medium through which one of God's promises to His people was fulfilled. David's establishment of a royal line, blessed and anointed directly by God, was a symbol of great power and motivation for the people of Israel: the kingship was the substance and means of the presence of God on earth. This was to have momentous consequences for the religious history of humanity, and especially so for the experience of the entire Western world. Because of it Jerusalem became the holy city and David became the prototype of an awaited Messiah. As symbol of the Messiah, the return of David, or the coming of David's "son," stood for the reassertion of the divine rule and presence in history: to judge it, to redeem it, to renew it. David thus became the symbol of a fulfillment in the future, final peace. In Israel's religious tradition the royal line, or "house," of David became a primary symbol of the bond between God and the nation. As in many ancient traditions, the king was thought of as both divine and human. The English word *messiah* is derived from *hameshiach* ("the anointed one"), the title of the kings of the line of David. Thus, in later times of disaster, Israel began to wait for a Messiah, a new mediator of the power of God who would redeem the people and their land. By designating Jesus as the son of David, Christianity underscored its conviction that this hope had been fulfilled. The son of David, in the figure of Jesus, became more emphatically a heavenly figure, the son of God enthroned to rule over the nations of the world. This was the matrix for the rise of Christianity.

*The Mysteries Unveiled by the Dead Sea Scrolls*

The Dead Sea is the lowest known place on the surface of the earth. It is a strange sea, so dense with minerals that nothing can sink into its waters, located in the southeast of Israel, south of Jericho, a land so dry that no vegetation would grow there if it were not for modern irrigation systems. The Roman historian and traveler Pliny wrote, "On the west coast of Lake Asphaltitis [the Dead Sea] are settled the Essenes, at some distance from the noisome odors that are experienced on the shore itself. They are a lonely people, the most extraordinary in the world, who live without women, without love, without money, with the palm trees for their only companions." On the northwestern shore of the sea there is a plateau, now known as the archaeological area of Qumran, once the city where the Essenes lived. Behind the plateau are a series of caves where in February 1947 the Dead Sea Scrolls were found by Bedouin boys who were playing in the rubble of an ancient Roman fortress. The scrolls, found rolled up inside clay pots, were recognized by scholars and archaeologists to be biblical and very ancient copies of the books that form the Old Testament. Because the texts on the scrolls showed only some minor variations from the texts in the Bible, their discovery, although archaeologically significant, did not make a great deal of difference from the layperson's point of view. What *did* make a difference, however, was the discovery of a smaller group of scrolls that are not biblical books, and the fragments of hundreds more, written about the time of the origins of Christianity. The titles of these documents are intriguing—*The Community Rule, The War of the Sons of Light with the Sons of Darkness*, and the most important and longest of all, *The Temple Scroll*—and their content reveals many strong similarities of ritual, thought, and Practice between the Essenes of Qumran and the early Christians. During the time of Qumran a great deal of Essene scribal activity was documenting a crucial period of history spanning approximately two hundred years, between 140 B.C.E. and 68 C.E.

The Essenes were a sect that rose like the Pharisees in the second century B.C.E. out of a conflict with the official priesthood of Jerusalem, and who consequently separated themselves from mainstream Jewry by forming a community at Qumran, on the northwestern shore of the Dead Sea. They preserved the priestly tradition of the house of King David, whose royal family had lost the throne in the fifth century B.C.E. and whose descendants had taken refuge at Qumran with their loyal supporters, and dreamt of the coming of the Messiah and of their restoration to the throne of Israel. At that time there were many Jews in both Israel and in the Diaspora who believed that only a descendant of

*The Ruins of Masada*, near Qumran in Israel. The Dead Sea is visible in the distance.

David could be truly king and return Israel to the society of old, and therefore supported the Essenes and their prophetic visions for the future.

The Essenes are not mentioned in the New Testament, but they were described by Roman and Greek travelers such as Philo, Pliny, and Josephus. Their founder was called the Teacher of Righteousness, and it was believed that he understood and interpreted the prophets even better than the prophets themselves during their own time. They practiced a monastic and secluded existence in the desert, far away from the ruling powers in the city and in the Temple of Jerusalem. They lived apart from society in constant study of the Scriptures and with a firm belief that they were the elect of Israel living in the end of days and to whom would come a messianic figure—a royal Messiah of

David. Membership in their group and acceptance or rejection of its founder determined their place in the age to come. Their leader, from age to age, had always been a direct descendant of the royal house of David, beginning with Nathan, one of the king's younger sons and the first of the Essenes. In the year 41 B.C.E., the time when Herod began rising to power, the leader of the Essenes was Heli, who two generations later would have a grandson: Jesus.

It was the rule among the Essenes that only after a long period of probation and initiation could a man become a member of this elect community with strict rules of discipline. Many rituals preceded most liturgical rites, the most important one of which was the participation in a sacred meal—an anticipation of the messianic banquet—to which only the fully initiated members in good standing were admitted and which was presided over by representatives of the Davidic messiahs. Although their communities were celibate, living "in the presence of the angels" and thus required to be in a state of ritual purity, they could marry for the sole purpose of procreation. After the consummation of the marriage both partners separated and returned to their monastic vows of celibacy, and the children were educated by priests. Their laws were strict, their discipline severe, and—unlike Pharisees, Sadduces, and Zealots—they were not simply different parties within Judaism but a separate eschatological sect. The Pharisees, for instance, also had lodges and a common meal, but membership in the Pharisaic party did not, as it did with the Essenes, guarantee a place in the age to come; and the attitude of the Pharisees to a leader or founder was not, as it was with the Essenes, one of the bases on which such a place could be attained. Thus, the Essenes were an eschatological Jewish sect, just as the early Jewish Christians would be later. The Essenes believed that they alone, among those living in the end time, would be saved.

Since the discovery of the Essene writings among the Dead Sea Scrolls many parallels have been drawn between this monastic sect and the early Christians: both met every day for a sacred meal of bread and wine to which only initiates were admitted, both practiced community sharing of property, both valued celibacy, both used baptism as a method of initiation, both were engaged in the war between light and darkness, and both saw apocalyptic visions in the future.

The significance of the discovery of the Dead Sea Scrolls is that these documents proved that in the Judean wilderness there lived a small community of mystics. The Essene priests interpreted the sacred scriptures in a mystical sense, devoting every hour of their lives to the shaping of the spirit in order to receive the Messiah among them and so be saved. They saw that hidden carefully within the words of the sacred texts of Judaism were esoteric and mystical meanings that could only be understood by initiates who had attained a degree of enlightenment. The Essene priests saw themselves as the sons of light, engaged in the cosmic war with the powers of darkness, a war that had begun in primordial times and that would end only in the last days of the universe. The Essene esoteric interpretation of the Scriptures revolved around the ability to see this struggle between good and evil. Their library also included many books of prophecy, such as the *Book of Enoch,* which foretold an apocalypse and extensively described the battle between the forces of light and darkness. Qumran and the Essene sect formed what many centuries later was discovered to be a Mystery School in the desert, a school that received pupils through rites of initiation in order to teach them enlightenment and that was directly linked to the ancient Davidic lineage preparing its members for the coming of the Messiah.

The Essenes of Qumran, mystic dwellers of the desert, practiced an ascetic form of spirituality that was later to be developed, albeit in a Christian form, by the contemplative tradition of the Desert Fathers for whom perfect prayer flourished in the solitude and barrenness of the desert. With the discovery of the Dead Sea Scrolls the idea that Jesus was just the son of a carpenter had to be abandoned: his background and his family bloodline would have made him familiar with the ascetic and mystical practices of the Essenes, and he himself would retire to the desert in solitude before beginning his ministry.

*Nazareth on 28 April 1839.* Plate 28 from Volume I of *The Holy Land,* engraved by Louis Haghe.

*Do you know me, Philip? He who has seen me has seen the Father; how can you say, "Show us the Father?" Do you not believe that I am in the Father and the Father in me?*

—John 14:9–10

*[Jesus declared,] "Come to me, all who labor and are heavy laden, and I will give you rest. Take my yoke upon you, and learn from me; for I am gentle and lowly in heart, and you will find rest for your souls. For my yoke is easy, and my burden is light."*

—Matthew 11:28–30

How interesting it would be if we could travel back in time to the year zero of the common era and find ourselves walking the hills of the Promised Land, the rivers and valleys around Canaan and Nazareth, their gentle slopes and ravines that hug a country of the soul, what seems to be a natural site for some sort of religious evolution. The Promised Land is a geographical and mythical blueprint marked from time immemorial on the soul of humanity; the Phoenicians, the Canaanites, the Hebrews, and the Christians would find its soil impregnated by the divine, a place where God and man reside in close proximity. In the desert around Beersheba archaeologists have discovered the superimposed layers of successive civilizations from Neolithic days to our own, each leaving behind their religious altars. This Holy Land was to become the seat of the most important metamorphoses of the religious spirit, of which both Judaism and Christianity would be the flowerings.

In that year zero of the common era, Palestine was under Roman rule and Herod was king. Although he was born on Jewish soil, he was not predominantly of Jewish blood: his mother was Arabian and his father an

Idumean, and neither of them were of royal birth. Herod's kingship was a reward he had brought back from Rome, and his rule was tyrannical, in service of foreign and pagan powers who had imposed their dominance over a nation dedicated to the one true God. Palestine's dissatisfaction under the Roman yoke was both political—the Romans could not essentially be part of God's plan for His chosen people and so they disrupted His work on earth—and spiritual—a nonhereditary king had taken the throne to serve a power other than the God of Israel. The Jewish people of Palestine tried to work under the Roman yoke as best they could: the Zealots through political and military underground intrigue, the Pharisees through spiritual and pacifist conciliatory attitudes toward the Romans and Herod, and the Essenes by removing themselves altogether to a remote community in the desert around Qumran.

An ancient prophecy written in the Bible by the Jewish prophet Micah told that a new ruler would come from the town of Bethlehem: *"Out of thee [Bethlehem] shall he come forth onto me that is to be the ruler in Israel: and his going forth is from the beginning"* (Micah 5:2). The great biblical prophet Isaiah said in the eighth century before the birth of Jesus, *"Behold a virgin shall conceive and bear a son, and his name shall be called Immanuel"* (Isaiah. 7:14). Bethlehem was the presumed birthplace, and certainly the home, of King David, the first anointed king of Israel, and so it would be only fitting that Jesus, a direct descendant of the royal family, would be born in the same place.

It is Luke, one of Jesus' disciples, who best tells us the story of the nativity in the New Testament:

*In the sixth month the angel Gabriel was sent from God to a city of Galilee named Nazareth, to a virgin betrothed of a man whose name was Joseph, of the house of David; and the virgin's name was Mary. And he came to her and said, "Hail, O favored one, the Lord is with you!" But she was greatly troubled at the saying, and considered in her mind what sort of meeting this might be. And the angel said to her, "Do not be afraid, Mary, for you have found favor with God. And behold, you will conceive in your womb and bear a son, and you shall call his name Jesus.*

He will be great, and will be called the Son of the Most High; and the Lord God will give to him the throne of his father David, and he will reign over the house of Jacob forever; and of his kingdom there will be no end."

And Mary said to the angel, "How shall this be, since I have no husband?" And the angel said to her, "The Holy Spirit will come upon you, and the power of the Most High will overshadow you; therefore the child to be born will be called holy, the Son of God. . . . For with God, nothing will be impossible." And Mary said, "Behold, I am the handmaid of the Lord; let it be to me according to your word." And the angel departed from her.

In those days a decree went out from Caesar Augustus that all the world should be enrolled. This was the first enrollment, when Quirinius was governor of Syria. And all went to be enrolled, each to his own city. And Joseph also went up from Galilee, from the

*Annunciation,* oil painting by Ernst Deger, 1835.

*The Birth of Christ.* Fresco from the Church of San Francesco, Assisi, attributed to Giotto di Bondone, c. 1315–1320.

city of Nazareth, to Judea, to the city of David, which is called Bethlehem, because he was of the house and lineage of David, to be enrolled with Mary, his betrothed, who was with child. And while they were there, the time came for her to be delivered. And she gave birth to her first-born son and wrapped him in swaddling cloths, and laid him in a manger, because there was no place for them in the inn.

And in that region there were shepherds out in the field, keeping watch over their flock by night. And an angel of the Lord appeared to them, and the glory of the Lord shone around them, and they were filled with fear. And the angel said to them, "Be not afraid; for behold, I bring you good news of a great joy which will come to all the people; for to you is born this day in the city of David a Savior, who is Christ the Lord. And this will be a sign for you: you will find a babe wrapped in swaddling cloths and lying in a manger." And suddenly there was with the angel a multitude of the heavenly host praising God and saying, Glory to God in the highest, and on earth, good will among men!

—Luke 1:26–2:14

Mary was at the time of the Annunciation a young teenager betrothed to Joseph, an older man. In the Hebrew world betrothal was tantamount to marriage, but the emphasis throughout the gospels is upon the mystery of the immaculate conception. A child was conceived in Mary's womb not through normal sexual relations—a virgin was miraculously impregnated by the Holy Spirit sent to her by God. Approximately seventy-five years after the birth of Jesus, his disciple Matthew was to rewrite Isaiah's prophecy of this miraculous birth in this passage in the New Testament: *"Behold, a virgin shall bring forth a son and they shall call him Emmanuel, which being interpreted is, God with us"* (Matthew 1:23). And it is again in Matthew's gospel that we read that another angel appeared to Joseph, who had discovered, much to his horror, that his wife-to-be was pregnant. Joseph was ready to break off the engagement, but the angel commanded him to see the marriage through, since the child in Mary's womb was conceived by the Holy Spirit. Born as the son of man Jesus' life would unfold in such an extraordinary way that he would become the Son of God. Jesus' miraculous conception and birth would form the context to later frame his adult behavior and religious calling. We must remember that the story of Jesus was first and foremost a deeply Jewish story, pregnant with symbols and images that pertained to that first-century Jewish heritage; the prophecies that foretold his birth, the circumstances of his conception, the favor he found with God even before conception were all part of the great constellation accompanying the presence of a Messiah.

Joseph and Mary lived in Nazareth, but the Roman governor of Syria, Quirinius, ordered at that time a census of the population of Palestine, and so Joseph chose to present himself at Bethlehem, his place of origin and the seat of his family, the royal descendants of the house of David. It was after a three-day journey from Nazareth to Bethlehem that Jesus was born, in a manger as Luke tells us, because there was no room for the family at any of the public inns due to the commotion of the census. The birth of Jesus in humble surroundings was, however, hailed by a comet appearing in the night sky, a sign that the future king was born, that was seen by the three Magi, who traveled to pay homage to the infant by presenting him with three gifts: gold for a king, incense for God, and myrrh for a mortal man.

According to Matthew the news of the birth of Jesus was not welcome at King Herod's palace; he was king of the Jews and wanted no rivals descended from the house of David, so he ordered all firstborn male babies to be slaughtered. Joseph and his endangered family fled to Egypt to escape from Herod's wrath. Historically, however, Herod may have died when Jesus was perhaps two or three years old, and Archelaus, his son and successor to the throne, struggled to keep political peace among the Jews. The Romans, who had trusted Herod to keep order, grew impatient with Archelaus's weakness in leadership and ruthlessly ruled that all candidates to kingship among the Jews must be killed, for they were all convinced that they were divinely appointed to rule Palestine. This decree would have included both Joseph and his young son Jesus, as direct descendants of David. They fled to Egypt in order to keep the bloodline intact and preserve their claim.

The birth of baby Jesus was controversial; from the beginning he represented a threat to the ruling house of Herod and a messianic hope to the royal house of David. His conception could be interpreted as equivocal, for Mary became pregnant with him before marriage, and even that was surrounded by strangeness and mystery. Jesus of Nazareth was first and foremost a small Jewish boy born at a time of religious and political unrest in Palestine. Underneath all the images of his time and place, he was also to become one in whom the eyes of faith perceived a "God presence." That experience, which would become the central mystery of Christianity, required an explanation. Jesus' person was an intersection where the human met the divine, he was a means through which people came to believe that God had been revealed, and his was a life into which people of every generation since were invited to enter if they wanted to touch that divine sense of eternity. Jesus the son of man was inextricably woven into his destiny and tragedy.

# Chapter Two

## Jesus of Nazareth

*In those days Jesus came from Nazareth of Galilee and was baptized by John in the Jordan. And when he came up out of the water, immediately he saw the heavens opened and a Spirit descending upon him like a dove; and a voice came from heaven, "Thou art my beloved Son; with thee I am well pleased."*

—Mark 1:9–11

*For now we see through a glass, darkly; but then face to face: now I know in part; but then shall I know even as also I am known.*

—1 Corinthians 13:12

SEPARATING THE HISTORICAL JESUS FROM THE BIBLICAL FIGURE—the son of man from the son of God—is almost an impossible task. Jesus was a human being, a particular man who lived at a particular time, whose personal history was inextricably linked to the political and religious history of his country, who worshiped in a particular manner, and whose view of God was shaped by a particular religious heritage. Modern scholars and historians in recent years have taken the task of placing this extraordinary life into its historical context and to discern Jesus' religious persona from the private self, distinguishing the few things we know about him from the huge forces and crucial influences that converged into and within him. This is a very delicate task because so many religious sensibilities are invested in the person of Jesus that even simple historical questions can be perceived as a direct attack on a believer's faith. In truth, we may never know who Jesus the man was, because even by the time the gospels were written he had already been invested with religious predestination and his disciples were perhaps blindly but certainly faithfully shaping his private self into a vehicle fit to convey a new message and a new religion.

From historical examinations we now know that his name was Yeshuah, not Jesus; his mother's name was Miriam, not Mary. We know that he worshiped at the local synagogue frequently, that he was familiar with the Jewish Scriptures, and that he spoke Aramaic as well as perhaps Greek and Hebrew. As a young Jewish boy he would have been familiar with the cultic traditions of the Hebrews and the social laws of uncleanliness. Some historians now suppose that as a direct descendent of the house of David he visited the Essene community at Qumran, that he and his family may have been part of the Essenes or shared in their messianic vision and hope. Certainly there is enough connection between the rites of the Essenes and the early Christians to support a strong link of faith between Jesus and these mystics of the desert.

There exists a thirteen-year gap between the accounts of Jesus' very early childhood until the time of his initiation, the year of his bar mitzvah. The only information we have on the holy boy's early years is in the gospel according to Luke, where he tells us, "The child grew and became strong, filled with wisdom; and the favor of God was upon him." The story of Jesus the man, however, accelerates when he and his family return to Jerusalem at Passover for his bar mitzvah, when he meets with the elders at the Temple. It was usual at the time for the rabbis to test the knowledge and engage young initiates in dialogues about the Law; Jesus surprised the elders with his rich spiritual understanding of the Scriptures and of the commandments. It was perhaps at this time that a seed began to flower in his consciousness about the mission he was to incarnate for the next twenty years of his life.

*And one of the scribes came up and heard them disputing with one another, and seeing that he answered them well, asked him, "Which commandment is the first of all?"*

*Jesus answered, "The first is, 'Hear, O Israel: the Lord our God, the Lord is one; you shall love the Lord your God with all your heart, and with all your soul, and with all your mind, and with all your strength.'*

*The second is this, 'You shall love your neighbor as yourself.' There is no other commandment greater than these."*

—Mark 12:28–31

*Das Jungste Gericht,* by Fra Angelico, *c.* 1431. Museo de San Marco, Florence.

The mystery of the Christ, the gradual awakening of God within the human person of Jesus, does not occur within any of the official settings of the Hebrew synagogues. As we read the progression of the gospels, we note that after the thirteen-year gap of Jesus' childhood, the mystery of the Son of Man suddenly deepens and the chronicles of his life events demand they be read more for their mystical value than for their historical content. We reach a juncture in all the gospels in which the actions of Jesus suddenly become imbued with mystical and spiritual force, as though his human frame had become hollow in order to allow for the revelation of his interior realm. Saint John of the Cross wrote several centuries later that Jesus was "like a mine with many abundant recesses of treasures, so that however deep individuals may go they never reach the bottom, but rather in every recess find new veins with new riches everywhere." We are pulled into the mystery of Christ even before the beginning of his ministry, the gospels progressively leading us through a series of events that are mysterious in essence, chronicling the awakening of the divine spirit in the Son of Man.

The first of these events that wakes Jesus like a thunderbolt is his meeting with a wild man called John the Baptist, a mystic and prophet to whom great crowds flocked to be cleansed from their sins by baptism in the waters of the river Jordan. According to the first-century historian Josephus, John the Baptist was:

> . . . a good man, and exhorted the Jews to lead righteous lives, practice justice towards one another and piety towards God, and so to join him in baptism. In his view this was a necessary preliminary if baptism was to be acceptable to God. They must not use it to gain pardon for whatever sins they committed, but as a consecration of the body, implying that the soul was thoroughly purified beforehand by right behavior.

John the Baptist was a powerful spiritual presence whose charisma drew many, his rites of baptism seeming to awaken in some Jews a hunger for the spiritual life that traditional Judaism was not supplying. John the Baptist had proclaimed that "someone more powerful than I am" would come to him, and when Jesus came forth John declared, "Behold, the lamb of God!" a clear sign that he recognized this messianic figure, a mutual awakening to the presence of spirit in the other that deeply affected both men. Baptisms were conducted in the river Jordan with people stripping off their clothes, entering naked into the waters, and being submerged completely for a few moments by the hands of John. As Jesus surfaced after immersion, he received a vision in the form of a white dove—a symbol that was to endure throughout the history of Christianity—accompanied by a heavenly voice announcing, "You are my beloved son; with you I am well pleased." This is the first clear declaration that Jesus is the Son of God, a revelation, an awakening, a belonging to a destiny that is not entirely human but infused with the will of God. The dove, symbol of peace and union and ultimately symbol of the flight of the pure soul to the heavens, is a vision that occurs frequently in early mystery initiations when a bird appears in dreams to indicate the willingness of the spirit to take flight. In Christian symbology, the dove represented the Holy Spirit descending upon the son of the holy Father. This is the moment when the seed planted by God begins to blossom at the heart of Jesus, releasing its sacred fragrance that infuses every act of the Son of Man, transforming it into an act of benediction and holiness. If we know little from the gospels about Jesus from the time of his birth to the time of his meeting with John the Baptist, it is because the seed was buried deep in the darkness of fertile soil, waiting for its awakening, waiting for the spring of the spirit. In this sense, John the Baptist is like spring rain falling on sown ground, maturing the seed,

*The Baptism
of Christ,
ivory,
c. 450 C.E.*

and his baptism of Jesus is the very moment of opening, of the blossoming of God within the human heart—John is the medium by which Jesus awakens to his radiance.

This event was to mark the beginning of Jesus' spiritual life. The next day when Jesus returns, John again calls out, "Behold, the lamb of God!" and two of John's disciples, Andrew and John the Evangelist, follow him to remain with the Messiah until the very end. Andrew found his brother Simon and brought him to see Jesus: *"But Jesus, looking upon him said, 'Thou art Simon, the son of John; thou shall be called Cephas [which interpreted is Peter]'"*(John 1:40–2). Jesus makes contact with a new disciple and immediately flashes the thought and the future mission for him: You shall be called the Rock! Peter was the man who went to Rome to bring the message of Christ and form the first small Christian communities that would in time dislodge classical paganism and establish Christianity as the dominant faith of Western civilization.

Baptism of
Christ, by
Pierro della
Francesca,
15th century.
National
Gallery,
London.

Immediately after his baptism Jesus retired to the wilderness of the desert for forty days of meditation and ascetic practices. Here again, we have the barrenness and solitude of the desert, where in prayer one receives from God true knowledge of God—*theognosis*. Jesus withdrew from his familiar surroundings in order to *know* the blossoming of God in his soul, allowing the fragrance of the holy to be released through his being. But solitude was not to be entirely blissful; the descent of the Holy Spirit demanded a cleansing of Jesus' soul, preparing him further for his mission:

*At once the Spirit sent him out into the desert; and he was in the desert for forty days, being tempted by Satan. He was with the wild animals, and angels attended him.*

—Mark 1:12–3

This is a time of purification in which the soul opens to receive the light of God, and as it does so, it lets go of the darkness and of all worldly attachments. This emptying of the spirit—known in later centuries as *kenosis*, literally meaning self-emptying—can be very painful and entail profound suffering, as everything that links us to the world of human perception and way of life needs to be expurgated. Saint John of the Cross, the Spanish mystic who lived in the sixteenth century, elucidated this process that all who embark upon the spiritual path go through, and likens it to a dark night of the soul, in which the human spirit slowly transforms into a vessel for the divine. Saint John of the Cross charted the progression of soul-cleansing in several stages, the first being The Night of the Senses:

*This dark night is a privation of all sensible appetites for the external things of the world, the delights of the flesh and the gratifications of the will. renounce and remain empty of any sensory satisfaction that is not purely for the honor and glory of God.*

*You should endeavor then to leave the senses as though in darkness, mortified, and empty of pleasure.*

This may sound harsh to our modern ears, but it is a process of detachment from all those things that hook our ego to life events and ultimately bring us suffering. It is a deep meditative process by which our consciousness undergoes both an active and a passive purification: today we may also choose to retreat, take a time apart for solitude and meditation—this is the active part of the soul-cleansing process. However, when we do go on retreats, something deep and mysterious happens at the very core of our being: we gain a certain detachment from all those things that crowded our lives with worries and fears;

we gain a different perspective on our everyday lives that is enriched by spirit. Jesus underwent this process in an extreme way, completely letting go and surrendering to the work of the divine spirit. Not surprisingly this deprivation of sensory pleasure—seeking emptiness in the middle of the desert—has its repercussions on the unconscious life, which sometimes rises in revolt. Zen Buddhism, for instance, speaks of a hallucinatory stage called *makyo*, literally "the world of the devil," when unconscious material flows to the surface of consciousness, causing torment to the meditator. Saint John of the Cross spoke of something similar when he wrote:

> *He [the devil] often purveys objects to the sense of sight, images of saints and most beautiful lights, and to hearing dissembled words, and to the sense of smell, fragrant odors; and he puts sweetness in one's mouth and delight in the sense of touch. He does this so that by enticing persons through these sensory objects he may induce them into many evils.*

This is the Temptation of Christ, his battling with Satan. Both Zen Buddhism and Christian mystical tradition offer the same advice: pay no attention to these images or lights or words or fragrances; let them go; remain quietly with the imageless wisdom that lies hidden in the inner depths. When one does not surrender to temptation but is able to remain centered and focused on meditation and prayer, the spirit is uplifted and rewarded with bliss and benediction, and perhaps this is the meaning of the gospel words *"and angels attended him."* Jesus underwent a purification of the senses in his dark night, and at dawn he found the sweetness of the life of the spirit as though angels, not devils, had helped him awaken from evil.

The moment of spiritual awakening linked Jesus and John the Baptist that day in the river, interlocking their destinies and histories forever. It was John's tragic death, in fact, that was to change Jesus' life. John the Baptist had spoken out against Herod and his poor observance of Judaic law, tradition, and rituals, for the king had married his brother's wife, Herodias. John's power and popularity with the crowds was such that he probably started a political and religious campaign against Herod Antipas and the yoke of Rome over the Palestinian people, and the king sent to have John arrested. It is in the gospel by Mark that we learn of John's tragic death:

*As for Herodias, she was furious with him and wanted to kill him, but she was not able to, because Herod was afraid of John, knowing him to be a good and holy man, and gave him his protection. When he had heard him speak, he was greatly perplexed, and yet he liked to listen to him.*

*An opportunity came on Herod's birthday when he gave a banquet for the nobles of his court, for his army officers and for the leading figures in Galilee. When the daughter of this same Herodias came in and danced, she delighted Herod and his guests, so the king said to the girl, "Ask me anything you like and I will give it to you." And he swore her an oath, "I will give you anything you ask, even half my kingdom."*

*The girl. . . made her request, "I want you to give me the head of John the Baptist, here and now, on a dish." The king was deeply distressed but, thinking of the oaths he had sworn, and of his guests, he was reluctant to break his word to her. So the king at once sent one of his bodyguard with orders to bring John's head. The man went off and beheaded him in prison; then he brought the head on a dish and gave it to the girl, and the girl gave it to her mother. When John's disciples heard about this, they came and took his body, and laid it in a tomb.*

—Mark 6:17–29

The followers of John the Baptist then went to the wilderness, *"like sheep without a shepherd who, with scant thought for provisions, immediately journeyed to a lonely place to seek out Jesus."* Apparently this was a large crowd of perhaps as many as five thousand men, a large following of his disciples who saw Jesus as both John's natural successor and as the potential new Messiah they so badly needed in the face of Roman oppression. According to John 6:15, *"Jesus could see they were about to come and take him by force and make him king."* The desert where Jesus had spent forty days, a wilderness around Jericho and south of Jerusalem, is rough and uninviting. Scarcely anything grows there, and it is devoid of any human habitation with only wild animals roaming. But this desert of solitude, far away from all distractions, was the perfect place for meditation and coming into close contact with God. A desert was where God first spoke to Israel at Sinai; the desert was where John, Jesus, and later Paul trained their spirits for the tasks that would be demanded of them; and a desert monastic tradition would grow from the followers of Jesus and continue uninterrupted until today. And it is in the wilderness that Jesus' ministry began. Rising to the people's need *"he set himself to teach them at some length"* (Mark 6:34), and he attended to their need by performing his first miracle:

> *Now when it was evening, his disciples came to him saying, "This is a desert place and the hour is already late; send the crowds away, do that they may go into the villages and buy themselves food."*
>
> *But Jesus said to them, "They do not need to go away; you yourselves give them some food." They answered him, "We have here only five loaves and two fishes." He said to them, "Bring them here to me."*
>
> *And when he had ordered the crowd to recline on the grass, he took the five loaves and the two fishes, and looking up to heaven, blessed and broke the loaves, and gave them to his disciples, and the disciples gave them to the crowds. And all ate and were*

> *satisfied; and they gathered up what was left over, twelve baskets full of fragments. Now the number of those who had eaten was five thousand men, without counting women and children.*
>
> —Matthew 14:15–21

The people were excited, for they saw in the miracle the sign of his messianic powers and thus insisted on hailing him as their king, Christ the King of the Jews. Jesus, however, wanted nothing to do with such royal titles and withdrew from the hysteria of the crowds, sending his disciples back across the Sea of Galilee:

*Der Wunderbare
Fischzug*, by
Konrad Witz,
c. 1444. Musee
d'Art et
d'Histoire,
Geneva.

*And when he had dismissed the crowd, he went up the mountain by himself to pray. And when it was late, he was there alone, but the boat was in the midst of the sea, buffeted by the waves, for the wind was against them. By the fourth watch of the night he came to them, walking upon the sea. And they, seeing him walking upon the sea, were greatly alarmed, and exclaimed, "It is a ghost!" And they cried out for fear. Then Jesus immediately spoke to them, saying, "Take courage; it is I, do not be afraid."*

*But Peter answered him and said, "Lord, if it is thou, bid me come to thee over the water." And he said, "Come." Then Peter got out of the boat and walked on the water to come to Jesus. But seeing the wind was strong, he was afraid; and as he began to sink he cried out, saying, "Lord, save me!" And Jesus at once stretched forth his hand and took hold of him, saying to him, "O thou of little faith, why didst thou doubt?"*

—Matthew 14:23–31

## Thine Is the Kingdom

Perhaps the landscape of the wilderness and the colors of the desert would metaphorically best encapsulate the simplicity of Jesus' message to the people: a striking and compelling call for simplicity, a state far away from complications, desire, and pain that is longed for by every soul and yet is so difficult to put into practice. At the time when Jesus was speaking, his words provided sanctuary, a rest from the vanity and the glory of Rome and its power-seeking appointed king Herod Antipas, and from the luxury-loving high priests of the Temple at Jerusalem. Jesus called for a return to the basics of the soul, for a realignment between the needs of the spirit and the needs of the body, for the cultivation of a simple attitude of mind: self-abnegation, shedding the earthly bonds of property, clothes, and family ties, and a mental attitude focused on dwelling in the Kingdom of God. His call, so resonant a contrast to the religious climate at the time, was in fact to become the eternal path back to the home of the soul—be simple now and thine is the kingdom of God. Jesus' message of simplicity was to be taken up from time to time throughout history by such diverse figures as Mother Teresa, Mahatma Gandhi, Saint Francis of Assisi, and even William Blake and many others who never rose to worldly fame because of their simplicity.

Jesus' simplicity, however, was enclosed within a deep mystery, a metamorphosis of the human will into a channel for God's mission on earth; there is an authority in all of the Messiah's actions and speeches that is not entirely human but God-infused, as though his very soul came from somewhere else or had entirely transformed so as to become an egoless mirror for God. How harsh the image such a mirror projects into the world of humanity. All the human faults are magnified in this reflection, and yet, it is only through taking stock of human weakness that one can begin to walk the path of beauty that leads back to the divine. When Jesus first communicates his intimacy with the Lord of Israel at a synagogue service, the congregation is shocked. Reportedly, Jesus read to his fellow Nazarenes Isaiah's long familiar passage relating to the promised Messiah:

> *The spirit of the Lord has been given to me,*
> *to proclaim liberty to the captives*
> *for he has anointed me.*
> *He has sent me to bring the good news to the poor,*
> *and to the blind new sight,*
> *to set the downtrodden free,*
> *to proclaim the Lord's year of favor.*
> —Isaiah 61:1–2

Many of those who had known Jesus as the son of Joseph since his earliest childhood were enraged by what they saw as his arrogance; not only was he proclaiming himself to be the chosen one, the Son of God, but he addressed the Lord as *Abba*, or "Father" in Aramaic, a word that carried a sense of familiarity virtually equivalent to "Daddy." Traditionally for Jews the name of God

*Christ and Mary Magdalen in the House of the Pharisees,* fresco by the School of Giotto, *c.* 1320. Church of San Francesco, Assisi.

was awesome and mystical and could thus not be set in writing or pronounced. From the beginning God's name was enclosed within the tetragrammaton, four Hebrew letters, the equivalents of YHWH, the custom being that when readers came upon these letters while reading passages in the Scriptures they would automatically substitute the word *Adonai*, Hebrew for Lord. For Jesus to use a familiar term like "father" for his God would have caused deep offense even to those he had grown up with in Nazareth.

For many others, however, Jesus represented a doorway into a new kingdom of religious hope, and the beginning of his ministry occurred in complete synchronicity with the need of the crowds to feel again the intimate presence of God in each of their individual lives.

Jesus, exhorted by the crowds and by the direct call he had received from God in the baptismal waters of the Jordan, began to preach around the shores of the Sea of Galilee. According to the Matthew and Mark gospels it seems that after leaving Nazareth Jesus had gone to live at Capernaum, a place that for a long time in history was nowhere to be found on the maps of Israel.

In 1866 a British engineer named Captain Charles Wilson identified the site the local Arabs called Tel-Hum on the shores of the Sea of Galilee, which had been called *Kfar Nahum* in Hebrew, meaning "village of Nahum" (Capernaum in Greek). Over the past two decades archaeologists have dug below the foundations of a Byzantine church found on the site, and have come across the remains of a large and yet more ancient private house dating to the first century and thus within the lifetime of Jesus. Unmistakably Christian inscriptions were found on the walls, such as *"Christ have mercy"* and *"Lord Jesus Christ help Your servant"* in Aramaic and Hebrew. This seems to have been perhaps the first house-church of the small community of disciples who gathered around Jesus, a place where people came to see him and hear his teachings. The practice of community living may have been borrowed from the Essenes at Qumran, and it became one of the chief features of Christianity in the centuries to follow, monastic enclosures representing one of the many ways in which the followers of Christ sought to find the intimate contact with God that Jesus had. By the fourth century, at the time of the Christian emperor Constantine, the house was brought down and a church was built upon it, the ruins of which can be seen today.

Jesus drew people who seemed to lack social status, perhaps in the same way as John the Baptist had attracted *"tax collectors and prostitutes"* (Matthew 21:32), because these were the people most in need of what he had to offer. The rabbis and high priests in Jerusalem and the mystics among the Essenes kept, in contrast to Jesus, a strict rule of distance between themselves and the congregation, maintaining their high status and privacy and the aura of mystery that surrounded their privileged contact with God. Jesus, on the other hand, broke that rule completely, closely associating with the tax collector Matthew, a man who would have been widely disliked because of his necessary collaboration with Roman rule, and with Mary Magdalen, *"a woman who had a bad name in the town"* (Luke 7:37–8). Throughout the gospel stories we hear of Jesus' immense compassion for those burdened

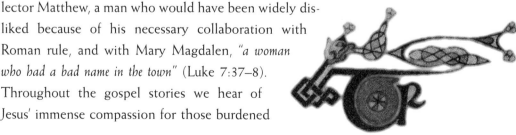

by pain—moral, spiritual, or physical. This is perhaps the greatest teaching of Christ and one of the most enlightening gifts he gave to humanity: he saw that the mystery of suffering was deep at the root of human existence, and inseparable from sin and estrangement of God. Suffering is the door into the soul that leads to God, and pain is both the result of sin but also the means of purification and return. Jesus did not avoid pain at any point as we do; he did not ignore it or insulate himself from it. He took people as he found them, with all their shortcomings, and voluntarily he shared their afflictions, their blame from society, and their need. This is where the immeasurable depth and breadth of Jesus' love lies, in the power of seizing reality as it is, embracing it in its totality to begin the healing process that takes each soul back to God, back to the Kingdom.

Part of the healing Jesus effected during his lifetime was through the embracing of women's pain and despair. In profound contrast with the priests and rabbis of his time, who would not even engage in conversation with a woman other than their wives, Jesus again broke the rules of a deeply patriarchal society locked into the degradation of women. In the gospel by John we read the story of the adulterous woman:

*Now the Scribes and Pharisees brought a woman caught in adultery. . . "Master, this woman has just now been caught in adultery. And in the Law Moses commanded us to stone such persons. What, therefore, dost thou say?" Now they were saying this to test him, in order that they might be able to accuse him. But Jesus, stooping down, began to write with his finger on the ground.*

*But when they continued asking him, he raised himself and said to them, "Let him who is without sin among you be the first to cast a stone at her." And again, stooping down he began to write on the ground. But hearing this, they went away, one by one, beginning with the eldest. And Jesus remained alone, with the woman standing in the midst.*

*And Jesus, raising himself, said to her, "Woman, where are they? Has no one condemned thee?" She said, "No one , Lord." Then Jesus said, "Neither will I condemn thee. Go thy way, and from now sin no more."*

—John 8:3–11

46

The Pharisees, the priestly and wealthy caste who dominated religious life at the time, were forever trying to discredit Jesus, setting traps for him to show his lack of moral and spiritual standing. An adulterous woman's acts were by no means accepted by Jesus, but rather put into context within everyone else's morality. Are we free of sin? No, no one is, and so he shows us the door to healing and to the grace of God. Another beautiful account of Jesus' compassion and mercy is to be found in Luke:

*Now one of the Pharisees asked him to dine with him; so he went into the house of the Pharisee, and reclined at table. And behold, a woman in the town who was a sinner, upon learning that he was at table in the Pharisee's house, brought an alabaster jar of ointment; and standing behind him at his feet, she began to bathe his feet with her tears, and wiped them with the hair of her head, and kissed his feet, and anointed them with ointment.*

*Now when the Pharisee who had invited him, saw it, he said to himself, "This man, were he a prophet, would surely know who and what manner of woman this is who is touching him, for she is a sinner."*

*And Jesus answered and said to him, "Simon, I have something to say to thee." And he said, "Master, speak." "A certain money lender had two debtors; the one owed five hundred denarii, the other fifty. As they had no means of paying, he forgave them both. Which of them, therefore, will love him more? Simon answered and said, "He, I suppose, to whom he forgave more." And he said to him, "Thou hast judged rightly." And turning to the woman he said to Simon, "Dost thou see this woman? I came into thy house; thou gavest me no water for my feet; but she bathed my feet with tears, and has wiped them with her hair. Thou gavest me no kiss; but she, from the moment she entered, has not ceased to kiss my feet. Thou didst not anoint my head with oil; but she has anointed my feet with ointment. Wherefore I say to thee, her sins, many as they are, shall be forgiven her, because she has loved much. But he to whom little is forgiven, loves little." And he said to her, "Thy sins are forgiven." And they who were at table with him began to say within themselves, "Who is this man, who even forgives sins?" But he said to the woman, "Thy faith has saved thee; go in peace."*

*Christ Healing* etching by Rembrandt van Rijn, 1649–1650. Detail from a larger work known as *The Ten Florin Piece.*

Jesus never romanticized sin nor did he side with passion against the law and order of Israel, but again and again in all the gospel stories he demonstrates that there is one thing more important to him than anything else: the individual, the human being, whether she be Mary Magdalen or Simon the Pharisee, and it is the individual who confronts God in Jesus. No mere prophet could have been a vehicle for forgiving sins; no mere mortal could have been perceived as a path that returns the individual to God. But Jesus, the Son of God *and* the Son of Man, is the living presence of the divine, and it is only with the understanding of this duality—the man in whom God is alive—that the crucial mystery at the heart of the gospels is revealed. In Jesus and in his interactions with people, from the poor to the very rich, God was present in an intimate, tangible, and human dimension. This is the greatest paradox represented by Jesus: he was born into a world that had worshiped one God for centuries and that viewed the divine as utterly transcendent. Israel had worked, prayed, and lived within a God-woven universe, swimming in the spirit like a fish in an ocean. With Jesus, however, the fish and the ocean became one; God and man became one; the spirit and the flesh became one. "God is here and thine is the Kingdom," Jesus proclaims to his baffled audience, and going even further into the living presence of the mystical dimension, Jesus shows that God is present in everyone, even the poor and the sinners, and that human suffering is the doorway into the Kingdom. The Judaic ideal of righteousness, of action directed toward God, is overthrown by Jesus when it leads the individual to a separation from God. For Jesus, God is not a matter of belief or moral conduct. God is a presence, a grace that descends upon us when we open our hearts—this is, ultimately, the meaning of Christian faith: to be humble, to be open, to simply embrace God now. Faith in Jesus is a revelation and not a mental idea of God's morality—God is as close and as intimately involved with the individual as a father, of the same flesh and of the same spirit, and the Promised Land is an experience of grace that occurs in every instance of life and in every human heart.

*Thine is the Kingdom* are Jesus' famous words for a world in need, spiritually crushed between the powers that rule the world and the remoteness of a God too transcendent to be of help in the depth of human suffering. God is to be found at the heart of the wound, close and intimate inside our flesh: *God is not far from each one of us, for in Him we live and move and have our being* (Acts 17:27–8).

## The Healer

*Now when it was evening, and the sun had set, they brought to him all who were ill and who were possessed. And the whole town had gathered together at the door. And he cured many who were afflicted with various diseases, and cast out many devils; and he did not permit them to speak, because they knew him.*
—Mark 1:32–4

Suffering is a shoreless ocean that surged upon Jesus, tide after tide. When the world around the Messiah opens its heart to him, it is a heart full of suffering, pain, and disease. Again and again throughout the gospels we read of the flood of pain that streams to Jesus from all quarters: from women condemned as sinners, from the blind, the lame, the possessed, the paralyzed, the nearly dead. Everywhere he looks he sees the manifestations of human suffering, of impermanence, of loss and grief. And he sets about to the task of healing—if there is but one activity that shines from the gospels it is Jesus' capacity to cure human suffering miraculously. Although acts of healing had been performed by Jewish holy men before and after Jesus, nothing in any of the Scriptures points to the healing phenomenon that this man from Nazareth became. He cured paralysis, lameness, fever, catalepsy, hemorrhage, skin disease, mental disorder, and possession by devils and bad spirits. In the earliest forms of Christian art, we see Jesus portrayed as working a miracle, often shown with a magician's wand in his hand. When he was asked by messengers of John the Baptist whether *"he was the one to come,"* Jesus answered, *"Go back and tell John what you have seen and heard: the blind see again, the lame walk, lepers are cleansed, and the deaf hear, the dead are raised to life. . . ."* (Luke 7:22). The leading Anglican scholar Canon Anthony Harvey of Westminster Abbey has pointed out the matter-of-fact way in which the miracle stories are described in the gospels:

> *In general one can say that the miracle stories in the gospels are unlike anything else in ancient literature. . . .They do not exaggerate the miracle or add sensational details, like the authors of early Christian hagiography [the lives of the saints]; but nor do they show the kind of detachment, amounting at times to skepticism, which is found in Herodotus or Lucian. . . .To a degree that is rare in the writings of antiquity, we can say, to use a modern phrase, that they tell the story straight. . . .*

Jesus walked a path of purification: with amazing compassion and grace he went about life curing the suffering and the sins of humanity. In touching the wounded heart of illness and disease—physical, moral, and spiritual—Jesus re-creates original life new and unspoiled. If Christ is the Way to the Kingdom of God, then the first step is about cleansing and purifying, the first step into what ancient mystical tradition was to call *via purgativa*, the purging of the soul in order to make room for the light of God.

The first step begins with a conversion of heart; in recognizing one's weakness and disease and in being moved by divine grace, one turns away from sin to God, who is love. For the two millennia of Christian history, sin and redemption have been the main bulwarks of theology. Of central importance is the story of the Fall. Created in the image of God, who was their friend, Adam and Eve walked naked and blissful in the Garden of Eden. They were one within themselves and lived in complete harmony with nature and the animals that surrounded them, and above all they were one with God. Then came the crash. Deceived by the serpent, they ate the forbidden fruit, only to find that they were naked, ashamed, afraid, broken, and scattered. They lost oneness with God and within themselves; they lost their bliss. Now they knew evil—their son Cain would rise up in anger and kill his brother Abel. Eve would suffer intolerable pains in childbirth; she would long for her man and Adam would rule over her. They would both toil and sweat tilling the earth, and they would die, returning to the dust from which they came. The universe fell with the man and the woman, the Garden of Eden a utopia long forgotten—this is the state of fallen nature and of original sin. But not all is lost. A redeemer will come, a Messiah who will save the people from their sins.

The grace of Jesus restores human suffering and transforms it into divine grace. Where the wound is most profound, so is the healing the most complete. What awakens us to the spiritual life is the vastness of the ocean of suffering: this is the beginning of the path that transforms human experience into redemption by God.

Jesus the universal healer teaches us that there is a web, woven by God, that catches us when we fall as long as we have faith in it. When Jesus tries to heal the sick in Nazareth, he is unable to do so because he is surrounded by people who, having known him all his life, have no faith in him and see him instead as an ordinary man gone crazy in professing to have direct authority from God:

*And all in the synagogue, as they heard these things, were filled with wrath. And they rose up and put him forth out of the town, and led him to the brow of the hill, on which their town was built, that they might throw him down headlong.*

—Luke 4:28–30

Even his mother Mary and his brothers try to stop him in Nazareth, as they too believe that he is possessed by madness. Yet, this divine madness and power to heal works everywhere else with those who have faith in him and in the workings of God through him. In the midst of the chaos caused by the mob in Nazareth, Jesus is still: *"But he, passing through their midst, went his way"*—a teaching of no violence in return for the violence his fellow villagers offer him. Again, the ambiguity of Jesus the man as the Son of God needs to be understood: divine power had flown into him and taken full possession, so that he had become a living manifestation of it. Modern historians have devoted much analysis and study to the historical Jesus, a naked figure divested of his garments of faith. The historical Jesus ceases to make sense in a mystical context: his miracles can be seen as mere acts of healing, the chronicles of the gospels can be seen as Christian propaganda issued by a cult threatened with extinction, and the man himself can, ultimately, be seen as a prophet who believed himself to be greater than he was and who died on the cross like a criminal. And although the historical analysis may well be entirely accurate, there resides a mystery wrapped around the mystery of this man. We must ask not only the historically appropriate question "Who was he?", but also the more pertinent questions of "How was he perceived by the people he affected, by those closest to him?" and "What is the Way of Jesus?"

Jesus, paradoxically, was not human and not godly, but both. And in defying the human and divine established paradigms he attracted wrath and worship both. Within that narrow margin there exists a door, a way into a Kingdom of healing and light that Jesus keeps pointing at, and we too can get through that portal when we find a balanced view of who he was as a mystic and as a man and are thus able to live his message in our everyday lives. The

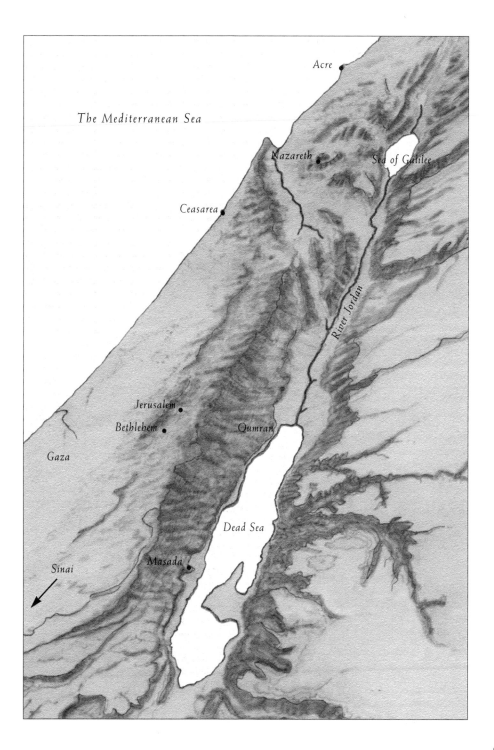

The Mediterranean Sea

Acre

Nazareth

Sea of Galilee

Ceasarea

River Jordan

Jerusalem

Bethlehem

Qumran

Gaza

Dead Sea

Sinai

Masada

53

"Zone of Jesus" opens up to us when we have complete faith that our suffering will be met and healed, when we knock at the door of despair and trust that it will open to us, when we believe that there is relief and healing on the other side of human suffering, and when we are in darkness and trust that we will see light. Within the Christian mystical tradition, Jesus was the very first to show that the soul can attain liberation if in the moments of darkest suffering we allow ourselves to trust completely and totally—this is the moment of salvation, this is the moment when God comes to our rescue, this is the moment when we are lost and found again. The importance of Jesus as a man is fundamental: his message is a living experience; his healing of the sick is a reality, and not an inspiring passage written in the Torah long ago by an enlightened prophet. Jesus shows us that we are not passively dependent upon God's grace, but that we can actively and consciously bring ourselves into his Kingdom, and through his teaching he makes it available as a physical, spiritual, and emotional experience comprehensible and attainable within the human realm. This immediacy evoked during his lifetime a totality of feeling in other people: those who had faith did so because through knowing Jesus they were transformed, their sins forgiven, and the doors to the Kingdom opened wide for them. Those who were critical felt no transformation in his presence and thus never developed faith in him. Later in the history of Christianity we meet again this all-or-nothing attitude toward him: Paul, for instance, a Jew who was extremely antagonistic toward the early Christian sect, underwent a profound transformative experience on the road to Damascus. In realizing the mystical meaning of Christ—a medium into spiritual knowledge of oneself—he converted to faith in Jesus.

*Come, Follow Me*

As soon as Jesus began his preaching and healing in Galilee, crowds surrounded and followed him, but a few men, entranced by his mystery and desiring to know him deeper, left their lives behind and became Jesus' devoted disciples. After John, Andrew, and Simon—the disciples of John the Baptist who were drawn to Jesus after his baptism in the Jordan—first made contact with him, they returned to their old occupations. But

> . . . *passing along by the sea of Galilee, he [Jesus]saw Simon and his brother Andrew, casting their nets into the sea (for they were fishermen). And Jesus said to them, "Come, follow me, and I will make you fishers of men." And at once they left the nets, and followed him. And going on a little farther, he saw James, the son of Zebedee, and his brother John; they also were in their boat mending their nets. Immediately he called them. And they left their father Zebedee in the boat with the hired men, and followed him.*
>
> —Mark 1:16–20

The circle of those who left everything behind to follow Jesus grew, even though until the very end Jesus remained a solitary figure, alone in his mission to teach others and alone in his profound intimacy with God. Jesus, however, selected twelve disciples to whom he would teach the mystery of the Kingdom of God:

> *And going up a mountain, he called to him men of his own choosing, and they came to him. And he appointed twelve that they might be with him and that he might send them forth to preach. To them he gave power to cure sickness and to cast out devils. There were Simon, to whom he gave the name Peter; and James, the son of Zebedee, and John the brother of James (these he surnamed Boanerges, that, Sons of Thunder); and Andrew, and Philip, and Bartholomew, and Matthew, and Thomas, and James the son of Alphaeus, and Thaddeus, and Simon the Cananaean, and Judas Iscariot, he who betrayed him.*
>
> —Mark 3:13–9

Among his closest disciples were also three women: Mary Magdalen, Mary of Bethany, and her sister Martha. Mary Magdalen, perhaps his most intimate friend, followed Jesus from place to place, while the sisters remained at home and welcomed him after his travels, offering him care and a place to rest away from the crowds. These were the women who in Jesus' deepest hour of need on Calvary proved to be more courageous than the men, who take his body down from the cross and embalm him with healing oils. His male disciples were always with him, sharing his experiences from the beginning of his public appearances to his ascension. At the beginning of the Sermon on the Mount we are told that he taught his disciples in a completely different manner from the rest of the people:

> *And seeing the crowds, he went up the mountain. And when he was seated, his disciples came to him. And opening his mouth he taught them. . . .*
>
> —Matthew 5:1–3

> *And when he was alone, those who were around him with the Twelve asked for the parables. And he said to them, "To you is given the mystery of the Kingdom of God; but to those outside all things are done in parables, so that seeing they may see, and not perceive; and hearing they may hear, and not understand; lest they should turn again and be forgiven.*
>
> —Mark 4:10–12

> *Jesus and his disciples went to the villages around Caesarea Philippi.*
> *On the way he asked them, "Who do people say that I am?" They replied, "Some say John the Baptist; others say Elijah; and still others, one of the prophets."*
> *"But what about you?" he asked. "Who do you say I am?" Peter answered, "You are the Christ."*
> *Jesus warned them not to tell anyone about him. And he began to teach them concerning the Son of Man. . . .*
>
> —Mark 8:27–31

Why the secrecy? What is the messianic mystery that Jesus only disclosed to his chosen few while teaching others through parables? Since his baptism and the struggles of the Temptation, the spiritual maturity of Jesus increases, his understanding of his intimacy with God deepens, and more and more he comes to own his mission and calling. As Peter and the other disci-

*Maesta,*
fresco by
Simone
Martini,
c. 1315.
Palazzo
Pubblico,
Siena.

ples acknowledge him as the Messiah, so he reveals himself to them, initiating them into the true meaning of his mystery. This is a teaching that cannot be taught to the crowds: the revelation of consciousness transmuted by the divine is a delicate and rare flowering in a human being, and its full essence can only be given to a few whose hearts are completely open to receiving it. Living, traveling, and listening to Jesus on a daily basis has prepared the disciples, has ripened them; their souls are like fertile ground on which the divine seed can be sown. They will be the ones who will be able to pass on the mystery to others, each one of them initiating a small group who will understand the mystery of Christ deeply. Jesus' statement that only those closest to him will truly understand while those outside will remain outsiders has little to do with spiritual elitism: his words express instead a leap of consciousness from the "outside" to the "inside" view. To the outsiders spiritual truths are like parables, teaching stories that reveal a kernel of truth. To those who are intimate, Jesus' words are an experience, an inner alchemy, a heartbeat with God, and a personal transformation.

The discovery of Christ's mystery stands at the heart of Christianity: it is possible for the individual to undergo the most profound flowering of consciousness, for a human body to become the receptacle of God's will. The title "Son of Man" denotes what we would today call a "principle" that can be realized within each individual. There is a seed waiting to burst forth; the way of Jesus is like gardening practice, preparing the ground of being for the flowering; the Holy Spirit is the descent of the light into the human soul and also the ascent of the divine within a human heart; the Kingdom of God is the all-permeating bliss of that fully flowered state of consciousness, the merging of the soul with God, the dissolution of the drop of water into the ocean. Each individual must be educated gradually toward the responsibilities of that freedom and of that flowering: he must first fully acknowledge the immense spiritual demands that such a transformation entails. Individuality with Jesus means mystical development, leaving all known territories behind as Jesus did—Nazareth, his family, his synagogue, even his known interpretations of the Scriptures, his religious background—and embarking on a journey into the unknown. Each man and woman must come to the awakening of consciousness by their own route and in their own time. Until that moment, the travails of the soul abandoning its attachments to the known principles of life must be conducted in privacy. This awakening cannot be thrust upon anyone: it must arise out of ripeness and out of the maturity of each individual soul. Hence the paradox of the gospels and of Jesus' words to his disciples: it is a truth known only to those "inside," yet it is a call to everyone to be shouted from the rooftops, a call to awaken every soul of the inhabited world to the possibility of transformation.

At the time of Jesus, the number of souls who were on the brink of such a giant step in awareness can only have been small. If Christianity had been the religion of them alone, it would have remained an esoteric hot house for the very few. Yet Christianity spread phenomenally throughout the ancient world, like a tidal wave sweeping individuals everywhere. To Jews this was a completely novel way of perceiving the path to God. This new consciousness was perceived above all as *salvation*.

## A Storm Gathers

Israel, bound by the Covenant forged on Sinai, was a nation that the prophets had taught to expect the coming of the Messiah. Jesus, however, presented a messianic dimension that was very foreign to the expectations of Israel. What the Hebrew tribe wanted was a perpetuation of the old Covenant, with God's dominion to be established and rooted in His chosen people, a deeper bond with the divine that would be brought about by a messianic event important only to the extent that it would eternalize God's promise to His people. The new Rabbi Jesus, however, never mentioned the Temple, nor the Kingdom of Israel, but questioned instead the world and the value of earthly existence—which for the Jews were blessed by God—proclaiming the divine government of perfect freedom. The Jews had been freed from the slavery in Egypt by God, who had guided them through their bondage and led them to the Promised Land, and thus they did not feel enslaved, but free and already blessed. Jesus and his emphasis on individual salvation and the one-to-one relationship with God was an alien spirit in the context of Israel; neither the Pharisees nor their hated rivals the Sadducees—liberal, progressive, and influenced by Hellenic culture—could rest until they had him safely under the ground. Once the waves created by Jesus gathered momentum and his movement became suspiciously powerful, they joined forces to put an end to the dangerous one.

What most troubled the Jews was Jesus' claim regarding his mission. When he taught in the temples all were astounded by his knowledge; they asked from where he had it, and who he was. But he produced no earthly authorization and simply referred to his being sent by God, his Father: *"My teaching is not my own, but his who sent me"* (John 7:16). Such learning, Jesus

*Christus am Olmberg*, oil on wood by Lucas Cranach, c. 1515–1520. Gemäldegalerie, Alte Meister, Dresden.

claimed, could be shared by anyone who entered in a deep spiritual bond with him from whom the Kingdom proceeded, surrendering his will to the Father, as Jesus himself had done. When asked where his father was, Jesus answered obliquely, *"You know neither me nor my Father. If you knew me, you would then know my Father also"* (John 8:19-20). The Father was hidden in unapproachable light and revealed himself only through his Son, with no other immediate approach to him; thus what was implied was that no one who was a stranger to Jesus could claim to truly know God, just as no one could know Jesus unless they opened their hearts to the Father and His chosen Son. As long as the Father and Son relationship was not fully accepted, the doors of the Kingdom of God would remain closed. When Jesus was asked for proof of this intimate rapport, he could naturally produce none except by the light of his very presence, but the Pharisees were blind to the light and saw only blasphemy, arrogance, and the workings of the devil. Enraged by this teacher who was hailed by the crowds as the King of the Jews, they sent henchmen to arrest Jesus, but these returned without having executed the order. The Pharisees asked, *"Why have you not brought him?"* and the attendants answered, *"Never has man spoken as this man."* The divine authority of Jesus was such that they dared not lay hands on him, to which the Pharisees replied, *"Have you also been led astray? Has any one of the rulers believed in him, or any of the Pharisees? But this crowd, which does not know the Law, is accursed"* (John 7:45–9). The Hebrew race at the time of Jesus was divided into a caste system descending steplike from the families of the high priests to the lowest "half-breed" offspring of a Hebrew father and an alien mother. Another sharp fissure ran horizontally, cleaving the entire nation into two categories: those who knew the Law, the tenets of right and wrong, and the mysticism of the Temple, and those who did not, the uninitiated and ignorant. The first group consisted of the intellectuals—the scribes and the Pharisees; the second of "the crowd." The most revered among the initiated would have nothing to do with what they considered the blasphemy and folly of Jesus. They considered that only the masses—ignorant and knowing nothing of Torah—would find good in him. The crowd was open to Jesus and his message, and the number of people who followed this new Messiah grew fast, posing not only a religious challenge but also a social threat to the higher strata of society.

Shortly after the attempted arrest of Jesus, another disturbing accident occurred, a sign and symbol of the dark storm gathering over him. He met a blind man in the street and felt compelled to heal him. He spat on the ground, kneading his saliva with dust, and spread the resulting paste over the blind man's eyes, and commanded him to go wash them in the waters of Siloe. The blind man obeyed and returned seeing. There was an uproar from the crowd. The man was brought to the Pharisees, who questioned him about the miracle. The story sounded impressive, and some sided with the man capable of such wonders, while others declared him not to be a man of God, but one who associated with the devil. The matter was then referred to the high council, who refused to believe that the man was really blind, and they summoned his parents, who testified that their son had been blind from birth. The high council still remained unbelieving, placed the man under ban, thrust him out of the community, and confiscated his property. When Jesus learned what had happened, he declared, *"For judgment have I come into this world, that they who do not see may see, and they who see may become blind"* (John 9:1–39). The Pharisees, for all their learning and wisdom, remained blind to Jesus.

Jesus' disciples were also thrown into conflict, for the Pharisees embodied the law and tradition of Israel, and their stand against Jesus made them fear for their own lives. Jesus' position was that there was no authority other than that which came from God, and those in power were but weeds that the heavenly Father had not planted in his garden—blind men's guides. Doubt from the authorities and from the disciples was like a shadow that followed Jesus wherever he went: he was hailed as King and Messiah by many, but many more also wanted him out of the way and considered him dangerous. How lonely and misunderstood Jesus must have felt, how great the task of lighting men's hearts must have seemed! Was this thorny path the only way he could have been recognized as a divine soul? Was his suffering necessary to reveal God's Covenant to the individual?

*The End*

Jesus, only too sharply aware of the darkness that the light of God was magnetizing around himself and his disciples, began to prepare them for his end in Jerusalem—for his death and resurrection: *The Son of Man is to be betrayed into the hands of men, and they will kill him; and on the third day he will rise again* (Matthew 17:21-2).

Jesus was painfully aware of his destiny and of the suffering that lay only days ahead, but was unable to fully convey what was to come to his friends. When the mother of Zebedee's brothers asked him to give her sons places of honor in heaven, Jesus replied: *"You do not know what you are asking for. Can you drink of the cup of which I am about to drink?"* (Matthew 20:22). The "cup" was his fate, proffered him by God; an excruciating destiny both on the spiritual level, as the failure to awaken humanity to the call of the Father, and on the human level, as extreme suffering and death brought at the hand of blindness.

Jesus continued his mission and performed the greatest of miracles in bringing Lazarus back from death. News of this traveled fast, and the Pharisees gathered in council to decide what should be done about the man Jesus:

> *The chief priests and the Pharisees therefore gathered together a council, and said, "What are we doing? For this man is working many signs. If we let him alone as he is, all will believe in him, and the Romans will come and take away both our place and our nation."*
>
> *But one of them, Caiaphas, being high priest that year, said to them, "You know nothing at all; nor do you reflect that it is expedient for us that one man die for the people, instead of the whole nation perishing."*
>
> *This, however, said not of himself; but being high priest that year, he prophesied that Jesus was to die for the nation; and not only for the nation, but that he might gather into one the children of God who were scattered abroad. So from that day forth their plan was to put him to death.*
>
> —John 11:47–53

*The Agony in the Garden,* painting by Andrea Mantegna 1431–1506. National Gallery, London.

Jesus then led three of his disciples—Peter, James, and his brother John—to a high mountain where they would be alone, and there finally revealed the mystery of who he was:

> . . .*his face shone as the sun, and his garments became white as snow. And behold, there appeared Moses and Elias talking together with him. Then Peter addressed Jesus saying, "Lord, it is good for us to be here. If thou wilt, let us set up three tents here, one for thee, one for Moses, and one for Elias." As he was still speaking, behold, a bright cloud overshadowed them, and behold, a voice out of the cloud said, "This is my beloved Son, in whom I am well pleased; hear him." And on hearing it the disciples fell on their faces and were exceedingly afraid. And Jesus came near and touched them, and said to them, "Arise, and do not be afraid." But lifting up their eyes, they saw no one but Jesus only.*
>
> *And as they were coming down from the mountain, Jesus cautioned them saying, "Tell the vision to no one, till the Son of Man has risen from the dead."*
>
> —Matthew 17:2–9

This was a mystery incomprehensible to the human mind. It merged the past with the present (Moses and Elias appeared as Jesus' friends); it merged the human with the divine; it merged the sacredness of the ancient prophets and fathers of Israel with Jesus, the controversial Son of God. The voice of God, thundering from the sky, gave full authority to Jesus as both His Son and the Messiah. The disclosure of this mystery was given to but three disciples: Peter, the strongest; John, the most loved; and James, the most spiritual. These three men received the vision of Christ in its full impact because the quality of their devotion was symbolic of the three pillars of the Church: strength, love and compassion, and spirit. Jesus was no doubt laying the foundations for his *ekklesia*, a Greek word that came to mean "church," but that translated literally means "community." The community of the holy is a gathering of spirits who have *seen* the mystery and have been touched by its light and force. This seeing and being with the mystery lies well beyond the capacity of the mind to comprehend, understand, and analyze. Had the disciples been taught in such a way that their minds would have understood everything Jesus was, the Church would have been built on the weak foundation of the intellect, trapped in its own rhetorical knowledge and unable to embrace the unknown. Jesus, however, taught by parable, by miracle, by presence, and by vision, bringing his disciples to feel and experience him fully. In following him they broke away from all previously known experience and stepped into the abyss of mystical vastness—there was no end to the wonder, no end to the intimacy with God, no end to the possibilities that opened for humanity when in loving Jesus they embraced his cosmic dimension. This vision that was to be called the Transfiguration of Christ is a symbol of the infinite dimension of the world of spirit that resides within every human being: Jesus showed his disciples the eternal, unbound Kingdom of God, where, bathed by divine light, we hear the voice of God confirming that each one of us is His son, His daughter. Terrifying though it was for Peter, James, and John, they were chosen by Jesus to undergo this mystical experience so that they would become, in every way, the foundation for his community after his death.

The sharing of such experiences was also highly significant: Jesus formed a small group of trusted disciples around him in order to teach them the value of fraternity. They slept, ate, and traveled with him at all times, and so over the years they came to intimately know his duality of godliness incarnate in human flesh.

Jesus once warned against domination of all kinds: *"But do not you be called 'Rabbi'; for one is your Master, and all you are brothers"* (Matthew 23:8). This was the beginning of the Christian "we." The faithful were to be bound to one another in mutual love and fraternity. They formed the family of God, in which all were brothers and sisters descending from the Father. The communal spirit was the ethos that characterized the development of Christianity from the very beginning—a sacred relationship between the individual, his fellow path-travelers, and God.

Jesus met his destiny full on, never for one moment attempting to escape what lay ahead. With his disciples he journeyed to Jerusalem, the holy city where all prophets and kings had died, to celebrate Passover; there he continued healing the sick and performing miraculous cures. Children and people in the streets celebrated the King of the Jews and everywhere cried out, "Hosanna to the Son of David!" The Pharisees asked him whether he approved the titles the crowd had given him—a blasphemy in Israel—and told him to forbid them, but Jesus replied: *"I tell you that if these keep silent, the stones will cry out"* (Luke 19:40).

The conflict was now at a head: Jesus was in Jerusalem, the enemy territory, and the Pharisees wanted him dead:

> *Then one of the Twelve, called Judas Iscariot, went to the chief priests, and said to them, "What are you willing to give for delivering him to you?" But they assigned him thirty pieces of silver. And from then on he sought out an opportunity to betray him.*
>
> —Matthew 26:4–5, 14–16

Jesus sent Peter and John to find a house where they could celebrate Passover and together they shared what was to be his Last Supper. *"Troubled in spirit,"* as the gospels tell us, he gave his disciples the mystery of surrendered love and union—his covenant and at the same time his command of love reiterated in this last hour together:

*This cup is the new covenant in my blood which shall be shed for you. . . . For I have given you an example, that as I have done to you, so you also should do.*

—John 13:15

*. . . that Scripture may be fulfilled, "He who eats bread with me has lifted his heel against me." . . . Amen, amen, I say to you, one of you will betray me.*

—John 13:18–21

*Now one of his disciples, he whom Jesus loved, was reclining at Jesus' bosom. Simon Peter therefore beckoned to him, and said to him, "Who is it of whom he speaks?" He therefore, leaning back upon the bosom of Jesus, said to him, "Lord, who is it?" Jesus answered, "It is he for whom I shall dip the bread, and give it to him." And when he had dipped the bread, he gave it to Judas Iscariot, the son of Simon.*

—John 13:23–26

Judas left quickly and Jesus remained alone with the disciples who were really his:

*And having taken bread, he gave thanks and broke, and gave it to them, saying, "Take and eat. This is my body, which is being given for you; do this in remembrance of me."*

—Luke 22:19

What followed was a night of fear and darkness and a dawn of death. After the Eucharist, Jesus and his disciples went to the garden of Gethsemane, where he commanded them to keep watch while he prayed. The power of God was no longer protecting the Son from his destiny; he had been left unguarded in the face of approaching death. His disciples fell asleep and did not keep watch. While Jesus was praying, an angel appeared to him to give him strength, but the shock of knowing what horrors awaited him made his body sweat drops of blood, his blood vessels having burst from the tension suffered in these for-

saken hours. Judas, in the meantime, arrived at Gethsemane with guards sent by the high council, and following the arranged sign, he kissed Jesus. The Master replied, "Judas, dost thou betray the Son of Man with a kiss?" Terrified, the disciples fled. The guards took Jesus prisoner and brought him to Annas, the high priest. Peter, by a device, managed to get into the gates of the house, but when he found himself accused of being a friend of Jesus he denied it three times just as Jesus had predicted during their Last Supper together. The disciples were distraught and did not know how they could have protected their Master.

Early in the morning the high council was summoned to accuse Jesus of blasphemy, since it was a crime punishable by death. Having tried him unfairly, they led him to the Pretorium, where Pontius Pilate held his court of justice. The Roman told them to judge him according to their own Jewish law, but the Pharisees, unable to sentence Jesus to death just before the Passover, wanted him accused under Roman law. Pontius Pilate saw no crime in the accusations shouted by the Jews, but when the crowd told Pilate that Jesus was worshiped as King of the Jews, the Roman judge sent him to Herod.

Herod was delighted to finally meet the Son of God and expected a miracle, a divine sign from him. But Jesus never said a word and remained silent throughout the king's questioning. Herod found him so obviously impotent that his interest turned into mockery, and garbing Jesus in a jester's royal cloak, Herod sent him back to Pontius Pilate. The Roman procurator summoned the populace and the high priests and declared that the charges against Jesus were groundless. Mystery and supernatural acts were not crimes in a Roman court of justice. Pilate counted upon the masses to demand Jesus' release, and gave them the choice of freeing either Jesus, King of the Jews, or Barabbas, a man imprisoned for committing murder. The crowds, at the instigation of the Pharisees, demanded that Barabbas be released, sealing Jesus' fate.

Pontius Pilate had Jesus flogged, believing perhaps that at the sight of blood the crowds would be placated. The guards put a scarlet cloak on him, lay a crown of thorns on his head, and placed a reed in his right hand, and flogged him. Again Pilate took Jesus back to the high priests, telling them that he found no crime in the man. But the priests replied that if he freed Jesus, he

was no friend of Ceasar, because Jesus was trying to overthrow Rome's power by declaring himself King of the Jews. Pilate knew that the Kingdom of the Messiah was not of this world, and repeatedly tried to free Jesus. But both the high council and the mob wanted him crucified, and so Pilate led him to his sorrowful destiny, declaring, *"I am innocent of the blood of this just man; see to it your-selves,"* and in so doing washed his hands of the whole affair.

The Messiah, after having been lashed with a pellet-studded whip, had to carry his cross to Calvary, the site of executions. Here, stripped of all his clothes, he was heaved upon the cross and nails were driven through his wrists and feet to hold him tight. The inscription "King of the Jews" was carved upon his instrument of torture.

This is the hour of deepest darkness, of most intense suffering of the soul. Jesus, completely abandoned, cried out: *"Elohi, elohi, lama sabachtani?"*— Father, why have you forsaken me? Jesus allowed his body to be murdered by

*The Last Supper.* Fresco by Domenico Ghirlandaio. St. Marco Monastery, Florence.

the doubt and fear of humanity; willingly, he underwent the most extreme ordeal. This was perhaps what Saint John of the Cross would compare to the second dark soul of the night, when the soul cleanses itself of all that is human and death hovers around threatening to take over. Jesus was dying on the cross, his disciples scattered and hiding in Jerusalem, too distraught to witness his torture. Only the women—Martha, her sister Mary, and Mary Magdalen—forever compassionate, remained at his feet. The end had come.

Roman practice was to break the legs of the crucified shortly before death, a measure that prevented the victims from raising themselves in order to breathe and thus accelerated their death. To prevent the bodies' remaining on the cross during the Sabbath, the Jews asked the guards to break their legs, but when they came to Jesus they found him already dead, so instead of breaking his tibia one of the soldiers pierced his side with a lance.

We don't know how long Jesus remained on the cross: Martha, Mary, and Mary Magdalen remained on Calvary throughout the ordeal and arranged for a rich man, Joseph of Arimathea, to take charge of Jesus' body and bury him in his new family tomb. Joseph provided for the burial linen and spices and oils, and the women, once Jesus was taken down from the cross before the beginning of Sabbath that evening, embalmed him, cleaned his wounds, and buried him inside the tomb.

## A New Beginning

*Now late in the night of the Sabbath, as the first day of the week began to dawn, Mary Magdalen and the other Mary came to see the sepulchre. And behold, there was a great earthquake; for an angel of the Lord came down from heaven, and drawing near rolled back the stone, and sat upon it. His countenance was like lightning, and his raiment like snow. And for fear of him the guards were terrified, and became like dead men.*

—Matthew 28:1–4

When the women entered the tomb, they found the body of Jesus gone. Mary Magdalen ran to Simon Peter and John and told them that someone had taken the body. The two men went to the tomb and found two angels in dazzling light who asked, *"Why do you seek the living one among the dead? He is not here, but has risen. Remember how he spoke to you while he was yet in Galilee, saying that the Son of Man must be betrayed into the hands of sinful men, and be crucified, and on the third day rise"* (Luke 24:4-7). Mary and Mary Magdalen and the two men ran to tell the others about what had happened. Everyone wanted to see the sepulchre, and they found the linen cloths lying inside the tomb but no body. Everyone returned home in shock, except for Mary, who stood outside her Master's burial site weeping. She then saw two angels where the body of Jesus had been laid. They asked her why she was weeping, and as she answered, she turned around and saw Jesus standing there. He asked her,

> *"Woman, why art though weeping? Whom dost thou seek?" She, thinking he was the gardener, said to him, "Sir, if thou hast removed him, tell me where thou hast laid him and I will take him away." Jesus said to her, "Mary!" Turning, she said to him, "Rabboni!" (that is to say, Master). Jesus said to her, "Do not touch me, for I have not yet ascended to my Father, but go to my brethren and say to them, 'I ascend to my Father and your Father, to my God and your God.'"*

> —John 20:4–17

The chronicle of the following days, the quiet and holy days of Passover, was a chronicle of disbelief, wonder, and fear at the risen Christ. His presence among the living disciples in mourning was strange; his coming shocked and terrified all of them; he no longer came and went but "appeared" and "vanished" with disturbing suddenness. Corporal limitations no longer ham-

*The Crucifixion,* Russian icon on wood, *c.* 1600. Private collection, Frankfurt.

pered him, and the barriers of time and space ceased to exist, allowing him to move with a freedom impossible on earth. In the gospels we read how the disciples saw him, felt his proximity, heard him, experienced his body's compactness, touching the wounds produced by the nails on the cross, and placing their hands on the gash at his side. He startled his disciples by appearing in the room where they were dining, they stared at him as though he were a ghost; then he asked them for something to eat and consumed the food before their very eyes.

*I write of what was from the beginning, what we have heard, what we have seen with our eyes, what we have looked upon and our hands have handled: of the Word of Life. And the Life was made known and we have seen, and now testify and announce to you, the Life Eternal which was with the Father, and has appeared to us. What we have seen and what we have heard we announce to you, in order that you also may have fellowship with us.*

—I John 1–3

These days after the Resurrection and before his return to the Father were full of mystery: What had happened to Jesus the man? Had he defied nature and returned to live after his crucifixion? The facts will always remain a mystery, buried in the strange events that occurred during these last days before the Ascension. The symbol, however, was clear: there was life after death, a life in which the spirit, unbound by terrestrial physical laws, could roam free for a few days before leaving the terrestrial plane completely. Probing deeper into the symbology of the Resurrection, we find that Jesus' teaching to his disciples was only complete after his death. After the cross, the Son of God lived between time and eternity, with the reaches of everlasting light unfolding before him, but he still passed among his beloved ones in transitoriness.

We discover in these disquieting Bible passages the "other" nature of Jesus: centered in eternity, he was divinely free, and came to us in essence. Jesus of Nazareth had finally crossed over to the other shore to become the Risen Christ, but before leaving our world completely, he returned to his disciples to instruct them as to how they should continue his work on earth:

*To them also he showed himself alive after his passion by many proofs, during forty days appearing to them and speaking of the kingdom of God. And while eating with them, he charged them not to depart from Jerusalem, but to wait for the promise of the Father, "of which you have heard," said he, "by my mouth; for John baptized with water, but you shall be baptized with the Holy Spirit not many days hence. . . and you shall be witnesses for me in Jerusalem and in all Judea and Samaria and even to the very ends of the earth."*

*And when he had said this, he was lifted up before their eyes, and a cloud took him out of their sight. And while they were gazing up to heaven as he went, behold, two men stood by them in white garments, and said to them: "Men of Galilee, why do you stand looking up to heaven? This Jesus who has been taken up from you into heaven, shall come in the same way as you have seen him going up to heaven."*

—Acts 1:1–11

And, after his Ascension, Christ endowed upon them his last gift, the baptism by the Holy Spirit:

*And when the days of the Pentecost were drawing to a close, they were all together in one place. And suddenly there came a sound from heaven, and of a violent wind blowing, and it filled the whole house where they were sitting. And there appeared to them parted tongues as of fire, which settled upon each of them. And they were all filled with the Holy Spirit and began to speak in foreign tongues, even as the Holy Spirit prompted them to speak.*

*Now there were staying at Jerusalem devout Jews from every nation under heaven. And when this sound was heard, the multitude gathered and were bewildered in mind, because each heard them speaking in his own language. But they were all amazed and marveled, saying, "Behold, are not all these that are speaking Galileans? And how have we heard each his own language in which he was born? Parthians and Medes and Elamites, and inhabitants of Mesopotamia, Judea, and Cappadocia, Pontus and Asia, and visitors from Rome, Jews and also proselytes, Cretans and Arabians, we have heard them speaking in our own languages of the wonderful works of God."*

*And all were amazed and perplexed, saying to one another, "What does this mean?"*

—Acts 2:1–13

The roaring from heaven was not noise in the earthly meaning of the word—it was a thunderbolt of awakening consciousness. The disciples underwent their final spiritual transformation—they were now able to speak in tongues; they made themselves understood by everyone. An ardent divine eloquence had settled over them so that they may tell others about the Son of God, calling everyone to the same awakening they had experienced. Whoever

*Noli me Tangere*, oil
painting by Titian,
c. 1511–1512.
National Gallery,
London.

heard them was profoundly shaken, for the Christian message was alive and
aflame; the disciples' light was contagious, a small congregation gathered
around them that received baptism, and the first fruit of the Church was born.

At first this congregation led a quiet existence, outwardly still embedded
in the traditional customs and ceremonies of the Temple. However, something
infinitely significant had happened to the followers of Jesus: a new faith was
born, and with it Christian existence. They had gained consciousness of a life
grounded in Christ that from beginning to the end opened people's eyes to a new
dimension—a new kingdom—of the spirit. The Covenant of God had been
accomplished for the Christian congregation. They believed that in Christ it was
finally fulfilled and that a New Covenant was established between the Father in
heaven and all who believed in him through Jesus Christ, a Covenant of faith
standing fast in a world that held it for scandal or folly. Now the promise lay at
the heart of Christianity, of a new creation that was about to grow, organically
rooted in the past and branching and flowering into the future.

# PART II

## IN THE FOOTSTEPS OF THE MESSIAH

# Chapter Three

## A Brief History of Mystical Christianity

*Thou shalt send forth thy spirit, and they shall be created: and thou shalt renew the
face of the earth.*

—Psalms 103:30

*There in the lucky dark,*
*none to observe me, darkness far and wide;*
*no signs for me to mark,*
*no other light, no guide*
*except for my heart—the fire, the fire inside!*

—John of the Cross

THE MARK OF TRUE SAINTLINESS IS TO LIVE beyond the psychology of one's day.
Jesus did this in his own extraordinary way, showing us that centuries of Judaic
religious belief, prophecy, and intimacy with God could be renewed by one
individual—a Messiah. He showed us that the greatness in each one of us is
manifested when we too live beyond the psychology of our day. Jesus taught
us that if God is present in the Son, so the Son is present in God, and thus
opened the doors to a completely new mode of perception and intimacy
between the individual and the Father.

In his life and acts Jesus brought soul and expanded the depth of the
mystical dimension of the Judaic religion at the time; in so doing he wrestled
with culture, religion, and political power, was banished, wounded, and ridiculed
as a mystic, and eventually killed. What he left us was a light, kindled in the spirit of his first beloved disciples who, slowly but surely, went on to kindle other
spirits, bringing a regenerated soul and spiritual context into a river run dry.

The story of Jesus, recounted in the previous two chapters, is a story that awakens our spiritual intelligence, tickles our mystical curiosity, serves as a reminder of our spiritual depth and resilience, shows us a spiritual journey, and reflects our own struggle with worldliness that is so necessary in order to unveil the power of the spirit. Above all, the story of Jesus sets an example: rich in metaphors and symbols, every event can be read both in its historical and mystical contexts, showing us facts about the times in which Jesus lived, and the parallels to our own times, to our own travails of the soul, to our own ways of deepening the intimacy with God. The story of Jesus is almost like another creation myth; it tells us of the birth of a Way of the Spirit, of a road that leads to the Kingdom of God, and it is perhaps for this reason that ancient mystics were prescribed to read the gospels at least once a week as a form of spiritual medicine. The story of Jesus provides an educational basis that informs our first childlike steps into the vastness of the world of mysticism.

*The Rebirth of the Divine Child* from the alchemical treatise, 'Elementia chemiae' by Johann Conrad Barchusen, 1718.

The word *mysticism* is derived from the Greek *mystikos*, which seems to have two basic meanings: "to shut one's senses" and "to enter the mysteries." Paradoxically these two meanings are related: one is able to embrace the mysteries of soul once one becomes disenchanted—and so shut off—from worldly ambitions and pursuits. This is the first movement of any individual who steps on the path toward God: the world outside no longer satisfies the hunger felt at soul level, and so a 180-degree turn is taken that brings us around to face the discovery of the inner world and the abode of the divine. After this process, the world outside is seen with fresh eyes. Knowledge of oneself is like switching on a light that shines on everything, highlighting its beauty, harmony, and perfection.

*Jesus on the Cross*, stained glass window, 13th c. Exeter Cathedral, Exeter.

For many centuries, however, the spiritual Christian traditions of the West focused on ascetic spirituality as a path of redemption from the original sin of humanity. What the West saw in its new spiritual awakening was not the beauty of the world, but its original and essential corruption, and sin was rampantly at work everywhere. Western Christian mysticism then was viewed not as an awakening toward the beauty, bliss, and goodness of the world, but as a path of mortification of the senses that went hand in hand with the debasement of nature—human, physical, animal, and vegetable. The only mysticism acceptable throughout many dark centuries of Christian history was the complete denigration of human nature, as this was considered the only possible way to completely purify the soul from its original sin and thus render it ready to enter the Kingdom of God. In clerical annals during and following this time, stories of the extent to which monks and nuns pursued the complete annihilation of the senses abound, and, frankly, they have rendered the term *mysticism* a pejorative in the West, making it synonymous with perverse practices of mortification of the flesh, a path so utterly uninviting and unpalatable that consequently there has been widespread disinterest in the cultivation of mysticism in the West. Today, not all who have been baptized as Christians find the Christian path an inspiration to deepen their knowledge of the spirit; many find that within the practices that have been inherited by our time, there is something essentially "missing." What is missing is what was cut off centuries before: the beauty of the cosmos, the joy of life, the bliss of life.

Believing that "shutting off the senses" in the connotation of mortification of the flesh is the only spiritual practice available within the Christian tradition is to embrace the very ignorance that led to those practices in the past. The Christian tradition is overwhelmingly rich in mystical exercises that recognize passion, body, and sensuality as part of the divine gift and of God's original blessing that graces our lives with awe and gratitude. A different meaning of "shutting off one's senses" can be retrieved from within the Christian tradition—prayer, silence, meditation, and spiritual retreat are the healthy and attractive alternatives to be found in many of the mystical Christian texts and exam-ples set by saints. Purification of the senses in a healthy context is practiced not because our senses and bodies are evil, but because much in our lives may not encourage a healthy, joyous, and happy balance in our bodies, minds, and spirits. In a way we eclipse beauty when we are so lost in life's problems that we no longer feel and taste light, grace, or joy but believe we have forgotten our innate capacity to live in beauty. Spiritual exercises are of immense value then, helping us retrieve our natural capacity for inner ecstasy, the contact with the divine, and the awakening of the Self. These tools are methods, mapped by exceptional individuals who lived throughout the centuries of Christian history, that chart the divine call to embrace the infinite bliss of God.

At the end of the first millennium C.E., people in Europe were still locked in the Dark Ages, and they welcomed the new millennium with a revival of interest in mysticism and spirituality. They believed that the natural disasters that were affecting their lives—plagues, comets, and earthquakes—had been sent by God as a warning sign that they should purify themselves.

The end of this current millennium is, in some ways, the opposite of the end of the first millennium. Both epochs are marked by an overwhelming upsurge of spirituality, a collective awakening that touches and transforms every aspect of life. The end of the first millennium was locked in superstition, fear of God, and repulsion and attraction to the devil. Ascetic practices flagellated not only the flesh but the soul in order to redeem humanity from original sin. By contrast, the end of this millennium is marked by light, grace, ecological spirituality, practice of community, renewal of worship, new images of justice and compassion, and a renewed spiritual education. Within Christian literature we can find materials that support these views: we find tales of a nun so holy that she never allowed herself to look at or touch any part of her body, and when she fell sick, she asked for permission from her spiritual director to wear stockings, since she considered it unbecoming for her naked feet to touch each other. We find stories of monks spending entire nights flagellating their bodies to expurgate impure thoughts that had wandered into their minds while in prayer, of priests so disgusted by the base nature of women that they never fixed eyes on any woman, not even their mothers, even though it was their duty to attend to them spiritually. These are sad stories that belong to the wardrobe of the past, and it is time they were shut off from modern mysticism forever. Now it is high time we evaluated the richness of the Christian mystical tradition and brought out from the past those tools, chronicles, and practices that are of great spiritual value to us today. Here we find enchanting and amazing tales of monks who practiced spiritual exercises that opened the heart to God, of prayer so deep one hears God whispering inside one's soul, of love so great one becomes a healer, of compassion so universal that it led someone like Saint Francis of Assisi to declare the sun his brother, the moon his sister, and the wild animals of the Umbrian forests that surrounded his monastery part of his spiritual community.

Embedded within Christian theology lie treasures—mystical pearls—that represent a fundamental heritage of our Western spiritual history. Unfortunately, since the age of Enlightenment the principles of Christian mysticism have remained hidden to the congregations of the faithful but luckily have been preserved on the outskirts of mainstream theology, cultivated in monasteries and faraway places where the pursuit of God was paramount. The philosophy of the age of Enlightenment, as a reaction to the obscure medieval past it succeeded, was based on rationalism, and it discarded mysticism, intuition, imagination, and cosmology as inappropriate to culture, education, and a religion that supported social and technological advancement. The view of the world and of nature was mechanistic; life was to be led according to Cartesian principles. The concept of "mystery" vanished with the deification of the machine. With the Enlightenment came the quest for the historical Christ, stripped of all his mysticism, magic, mystery, and symbology. The historical Christ that was left after all the scientific investigations was but a shadow of his former self, and so, no longer interesting as a paradigm that helped to awaken the consciousness of humanity, he came to be progressively discarded as no longer worthy of inspiration, and the scientific exploration of the "true Jesus" was hailed as the new truth. The loss of a theology that preserved the mystical Christ consequently entailed a deep rupture and a frightening alienation between the faithful and their heritage. Unknown to the people who prayed and believed in God, the source of nourishment for their spirit had been banished from their everyday life and replaced with a culture that firmly disbelieved any mystery, any magic, any illumination of the inner world. Rationalism was to be the new food for the soul from the seventeenth century onward. The early incandescence that Jesus had brought to his disciples and that they in turn transmitted to others so effectively as to make Christianity the primary religion of the West was extinguished with the age of rationalism. The hunger of the spirit, however, is not easily quenched, and although it may be suppressed for centuries, it inevitably resurfaces at some later date with renewed and greater pangs. Now is the time for us to attend to our hungry souls and to recover the lost mystical heritage that will feed them. In his passionate call for a retrieval of our lost spiritual selves, author and priest Matthew Fox has outlined how we should address our needs in order to satisfy that hunger:

*Mary, Mother of God.* Icon painted on wood, 13th c. Tretyakov Gallery, Moscow.

*I believe the issue today for the third millennium of Christianity—if the earth is to survive into the next century—is the* quest *for the Cosmic Christ. The movement from the Enlightenment's quest for the historical Jesus to today's quest for the Cosmic Christ names the paradigm shift that religion and theology presently need to undergo. One cannot explore the meaning and power of the Cosmic Christ without a living cosmology, a living mysticism, and the spiritual discipline of art as meditation. The holy trinity of science (knowledge of creation), mysticism (experiential union with creation and its unnameable mysteries), and art (expression of our awe at creation) is what constitute a living cosmology. Every theologian must embark on these pathways and awaken them within if the theological enterprise is to accomplish its task in our time. This will require a deep letting go of the old paradigms of education and theology.*

—Matthew Fox, The Coming of the Cosmic Christ

Matthew Fox identifies the Cosmic Christ as a mystical paradigm that can be sourced to the preexistent wisdom of Israel, and represents a dimension known and explored by mystics as far back as the prophets of the Old Testament all the way across the centuries to the Greek Fathers and the medieval West. Teilhard de Chardin in his book *Heart* called the Cosmic Christ the "third" nature of Christ, meaning that it takes us beyond the fourth-century conciliar definitions of Christ's human and divine natures into a third realm, "neither human nor divine, but cosmic." After the Middle Ages, with the progressive thrust of culture toward the age of Enlightenment, the Cosmic Christ fades until he becomes invisible, his image preserved only at the periphery of official theology.

In order to explore the dimensions of modern Christian mysticism and how it can be developed in all its forms, we need to return to its sources and understand the rich heritage that Christianity has kept buried in her bosom for centuries. The following sections present the basic recovery of the principles of mystical Christianity, beginning with the disciples after the Ascension and concluding with medieval mystics.

## The Unfolding of the Primitive Church

In the beginning Christianity as continued by the disciples of Jesus and their converts was not yet known as "Christian." The early congregation was Jewish, the sayings of Jesus had not yet been written down, and his message and vision were passed on orally to the new faithful. During his ministry, Jesus was the leader of a sect movement within Judaism. During his lifetime and through his crucifixion there was little that separated the disciples from their fellow Jews. The Ascension, however, was to change radically the nature of Jesus' following.

*Christ in Glory,* Russian icon, 19th c.

When Christ arose from the dead, he appeared repeatedly to his disciples and after forty days was taken by a light up to heaven to return to the Kingdom of his Father—these were the mystical events that would forever distance the movement from every other Jewish sect of the past or of the future. Although it took time for the fact to be recognized fully, beginning with the Resurrection the disciples were participants in a new religion, one that added far too much new culture to Judaism to be an internal sect any longer. Of course, the complete break between church and synagogue took centuries, even though Jewish authorities in Jerusalem labeled the followers of Jesus as heretics beyond the boundaries of the community from the very beginning. When historians speak of the *early* Church, they do not mean the church gatherings of the disciples in Jerusalem, but the Pauline Church as founded in Rome by Paul the Apostle, for this was the church that triumphed and changed history.

The disciples, true to their calling, began to travel outside the bounds of Israel transmitting the message of the risen Christ. The Jews of the Diaspora far outnumbered the Jews living in Palestine and were greatly influenced by Greek culture and philosophy. Their wealth, urban lifestyle, language, and occupations made them marginal participants in the orthodox religious ways of Palestine. They read, spoke, thought, and worshiped in Greek, and subsequent to their constant contact with the polytheistic religions of the countries they inhabited, they absorbed many elements of paganism. Ethnically they remained Jews, but they were separated from the Law of the Torah and the customs of Israel's synagogues. The new sect of Christians, by offering both a cultural continuity with Israel and a new development on the prophecies in the Scriptures, became vastly attractive to Jews in the Diaspora.

For Hellenized Jews, pregnant with Platonic philosophy, the mysticism of Jesus was more readily embraceable than the thundering and jealous Yahweh of the Old Testament. The seemingly abstract concepts of the parables of Jesus were better understood and were more palatable to the Greek mind than the endless restrictions imposed on life by the Torah. The first significant converts to Christianity were not Jews from Palestine or Gentiles, but

Diaspora Jews who broke away from orthodoxy to join the new sect. The name Christianity began to denote, over years of formative development, that religious stream that had detached itself from Judaism to form a new river. The first Christians were nonpracticing Jews who found renewal in the new Messiah.

The first Christian communities, born out of the disciples' efforts, were concentrated in the East—in Asia Minor, Egypt, and North Africa—the areas of the Jewish Diaspora. Alexandria of Egypt, the capital of Hellenism and Judaism, became the home of the largest Christian congregation. In the cities of the East the proportion of Christians grew steadily, and the communities, over time, began to baptize and include Gentiles in the new religion. It was predominantly an urban religious interest—hence the term *paganus* or "countryman" came to denote non-Christians (pagans). The Christian communities of the East were the foundation for the development of the Eastern Church, also known to us today as the Christian Orthodox Church ("orthodox" meaning "right believing").

The apostle Paul, who had never known Jesus and had sided with Jewish wrath against the Christian sect, was converted when he underwent a transforming experience that opened his heart to Christ on the road to Damascus. Paul set up several congregations in the East, relaxed the rules to accept Gentiles, and was the most ardent promoter of the early Church. It is perhaps due entirely to his own efforts that the communities took root and expanded, spreading the Christian message far and wide. Paul went back and forth between Jerusalem, his spiritual home, and the various communities he had set up. While in Jerusalem he was mistakenly accused of bringing one of the Gentile delegates into the inner courts of the Temple, beyond the barrier excluding Gentiles. He was arrested, partly to save his life from the mob, but treated well because of his Roman citizenship. When a plot against his life came to light, he was removed to Caesarea, the Roman military headquarters. The governor Felix kept him in prison to avoid antagonizing the Jewish authorities. Two years later Felix's successor, Festus, wanted to send him to Jerusalem for trial, but Paul refused to go and appealed to Caesar. It is by these unfortunate circumstances that Paul arrived in Rome, the

capital of the empire, in the year 60, and it was in Rome that his work would flower beyond anyone's expectation, making the original message of Jesus into the dominant religious force in the West.

Early Christianity thus spread across the Greco-Roman world, creating by the second century C.E. churches in cities such as Caesarea Maritima, Damascus, Antioch, Alexandria, Smyrna, Athens, Corinth, Ephesus, Rome, Memphis, Syracuse, and Carthage. The historian Ronald Hock estimates that Paul covered nearly ten thousand miles on his mission. And Wayne Meeks, in his book *The First Urban Christians*, partly attributes the rate of success of Christianity to the fact that "the people of the Roman Empire traveled more extensively and more easily than anyone before them did or would again until the nineteenth century." This fact alone implies that not only people but ideas, specifically *religious* ideas, also traveled easily across the empire, influencing many in their wake. The Romans were known for being superstitious but not overly religious, and they incorporated gods and goddesses from every country they conquered into their own pantheon.

Rodney Stark, professor of sociology and comparative religion at the University of Washington, successfully argues in his book *The Rise of Christianity* that the Jesus movement became dominant because it was simply in the right place at the right time—in effect it rode the tidal wave caused by the forces that rocked the Roman Empire. Historians now conclude that the fall of the empire was not caused by the "moral decadence" of its capital and senate, but by two great epidemics that swept across Europe during the second century. Imported from the East, a first epidemic of what is thought to have been smallpox killed a vast portion of the population. Almost a century later a second terrible epidemic struck the Roman world, causing widespread crisis and calamity. With mortality rates mounting dramatically during these two disasters, large numbers of people became disconnected and torn apart from the fabric of family and society that had held them together. With the bonds loosened, Christianity provided a new attachment to replace the old ones. Rodney Stark shows that it is at times of despair such as these that a new religion may arise to revitalize the soul of a culture in collapse:

*Apostle Paul*,
wall painting
of Greco-
Serbian origin,
*c.* 1340.
Church of the
Ascension of
Christ,
Decani.

*Frequently in human history, crises produced by natural or social disasters have been translated into crises of faith. Typically this occurs because the disaster places demands upon the prevailing religion that it appears unable to meet. This inability can occur at two levels. First, the religion may fail to provide a satisfactory explanation of why the disaster occurred. Second, the religion may seem to be* unavailing *against the disaster, which becomes truly critical when all nonreligious means also prove inadequate—when the supernatural remains the only plausible Source of help. In response to these "failures" of their traditional faiths, societies frequently have evolved or adopted new faiths.*

William McNeill in his book *Plagues and Peoples* suggests that Christianity offered spiritual sanctuary and answers in a world gone awry: *Another advantage Christians enjoyed over pagans was that the teaching of their faith made life meaningful even amid sudden and surprising death. . . . Even a shattered remnant of survivors who had somehow made it through war or pestilence or both could find warm, immediate and healing consolation in the vision of a heavenly existence for those missing relatives and friends. . . Christianity was, therefore, a system of thought and feeling thoroughly adapted to a time of troubles in which hardship, disease, and violent death commonly prevailed.*

Even though Christians were persecuted and tortured in Rome for refusing to comply with the pagan sacrificial practices to Roman gods that were believed to ensure the power of the empire, the small faith grew and grew. Professor Rodney Stark speculates that "in an empire having a population of at least 60 million, there might well have been 33 million Christians by 350." This fact alone may have been the primary cause that led to the end of the persecutions—Christians represented half the empire—and Emperor Constantine came to embrace the new faith as his own religion. Shirley Jackson Case, in her paper titled "The Acceptance of Christianity by the Roman Emperors," notes that attempts by Emperor Diocletian in 303 and by his successor Galerius in 305 to use persecutions and torture to force the Christians to sacrifice for Roman gods failed because "by the year 300

Christianity had become too widely accepted in Roman society to make possible a successful persecution on the part of the government." In examining Constantine's edict of toleration for Christianity, Jackson Case shows that Emperor Constantine's conversion was less a matter of his own faith in God than a practical alignment of state policy with the reality of the time:

> *In this document one perceives very easily the real basis of Constantine's favor for Christianity. First, there is the characteristic attitude of an emperor who is seeking supernatural support for his government, and secondly, there is a recognition of the fact that the Christian element in the population is now so large, and its support for Constantine and Licinius in their conflict with rivals who still opposed Christianity, is so highly esteemed, that the emperors are ready to credit the Christian god with the exercise of a measure of supernatural power on a par with the other gods of the State.*

The early Christian Church was known as *ekklesia*, a Greek word meaning "community" that denotes the character of those primitive gatherings of both Jews and Gentiles living in the empire at the beginning of the first millennium. Culture was infused with both Latin and Greek philosophy and pagan thought, some of which was naturally absorbed by the Christians. Educated Christians shared this literary, philosophical, and cultural tradition with educated pagans. The defenders of Christianity against pagan attack (especially Justin Martyr and Clement of Alexandria in the second century) welcomed classical philosophy and literature; they wished only to reject all polytheistic myth and cult and all metaphysical and ethical doctrines irreconcilable with Christian belief. Clement of Alexandria, second known head of the catechetical school at Alexandria, possessed a wide erudition in the major classics and knew the works of Plato and Homer intimately. His successor at Alexandria, Origen, showed less interest in literary and aesthetic matters but was a greater scholar and thinker; he was the first to apply the methods of Alexandrian philology to the text of the Bible. Thus the teachings that Jesus had imparted to his disciples in Galilee—the fishermen, tax collectors, and women of ill repute—were inherited by the immensely sophisticated Greco-Roman world.

The new setting brought new ethics into the Christian message. It was hard for Christians to attack paganism and not seem appalled by the totality of classical culture and the imperial government. The hope of the earliest Church was to build into its ethic a deep detachment from this world's goods—the pagan goods—no matter how esteemed. This was done to preserve the purity of Christ. This detachment deemed celibacy superior to marriage and renounced pretensions to high culture. The passionate urgency of the Christian mission did not allow distractions, an attitude that stamped any serious interest in Science, history, or belles letres with the stigma of worldliness. This detachment from the world, born out of an effort to preserve a new religion that could so easily have been driven to extinction by outside cultural forces, became the modus operandi of the Church throughout the centuries to come. Detachment was especially cultivated in the monastic tradition, but for many centuries Science was believed by the Church and its lay adherents to be evil and against the spirit. It is only now, in the latter part of the twentieth century, that for the first time in nearly two millennia of Christian history we are undergoing a profound paradigm shift when considering the effects of the Christian detachment. Now science and religion are joining hands once more to explain the mystical qualities contained in every cell of our universe. In a post-Newtonian science and in a post-Augustinian theology the cosmic principles that were first unveiled as mystical pearls by Jesus are now finally making sense. For instance, the cosmic principle of interdependence is now seen as a basic law of our universe. The German saint Hildegard of Bingen, who lived in the twelfth century, expressed this same principle in spiritual terms: "God has arranged all things in the world in consideration of everything else." Scientist Brian Swimme says that to take in a deep breath is to breathe in some of the breath that Jesus breathed on the cross—this is interdependence. Today mystics and scientists alike are urging us to a new level of consciousness, a new awareness of the interdependence of things. To acknowledge this new scientific and mystical thought would transform and re-create all our institutions and systems—nations, economics, politics, worship, education—in order to *righten* relationships, which is the true meaning of righteousness in the Scriptures.

The primitive Church, however, could only escape extinction by fighting the battles it faced in the old ways. From the very beginning, the attitude of the Christians toward other religions (except Judaism) was generally very negative. All forms of paganism—the Oriental mystery religions of Isis, Attis, Adonis, and Mithra as well as the ancient cults of classical Greece and Rome—were regarded as the cults of evil spirits. With the exception of the notion of baptism as a rebirth, Christians generally and significantly avoided the characteristic vocabularies of the mystery religions. The mysteries of Isis, Attis, Adonis, and Mithra were basically fertility rites to ensure good crops, and they answered to needs different from those addressed by the Christian gospel. The main difference between Christianity and the pagan cults consisted in the tolerant attitude of the latter: initiation into the mysteries of Isis did not mean renouncing allegiance to Apollo or Attis, whereas Christian baptism required complete conversion to monotheism and exclusive devotion. Many converts naturally brought old attitudes with them into the Church. Amulets and peasant superstitions were for centuries the object of critical attention by the clergy. The Christians tried to provide counterattractions by placing Christian festivals on the same days of the year as pagan feasts. Solar monotheism was popular in late third-century paganism, and soon the Western churches were keeping the winter solstice (December 25) as Christ's Nativity—the East kept January 6. Midsummer Day was Replaced by the feast of John the Baptist. Only Easter, celebrating Christ's Resurrection, and Pentecost, marking the advent of the Holy Spirit, were feasts owing nothing to Gentile analogies for their origin; they both were derived from Jewish feasts. From the fifth century C.E. on, great pagan temples, such as the Parthenon in Athens, were gradually transformed into Christian churches.

*The Eastern and Western Churches*

Constantine the Great, declared emperor of the Roman Empire at York, Britain in 306 C.E., converted to Christianity in 312, became sole emperor in 324, and founded the city of Constantinople in 330, just seven years before his death. During his time he was regarded as a great revolutionary, especially in religion. Although he did not make Christianity the religion of the empire, his foundation of Constantinople—conceived as the new Rome—as a Christian city profoundly affected the future political and ecclesiastical structure of the new religion. After his death the empire was rocked by deep inflation, epidemic plagues, and unrest among the people. These were the most weakening factors before the barbarian invasions of the fifth century that were finally to destroy the great power of the West.

Constantine brought the Church out of its withdrawal from the world to accept social responsibility, and helped pagan society to be won for the Church. On both sides, the alliance of the Church and emperor evoked opposition, which among the Christians emerged in the monks' retirement to the desert. This was the first real split between the *ekklesia* as brought by the disciples from Israel and the establishment of a monastic tradition within Christianity. Those who sought real mysticism, untainted by worldly ambitions, retired to the desert, as Jesus had done so long before in order to find communion with God through ascetic practices. Away from the Church that accommodated and adapted itself to the politics of the emperors, the desert fathers, of whom Saint Anthony is the primary representative of that time, lived in huts and caves in the desert of Egypt. Their whole lives were directed to seeking God through prayer, meditation, austerity, and manual work. They were consulted by laypeople on matters of the soul, and seekers would undertake long journeys to the hermitages of these holy men, a practice still maintained today.

The quietly mounting pressure against paganism in the fourth century culminated in the decrees of Emperor Theodosius I (reigned 379-95), who made orthodox Christianity an essential requirement of good citizenship, and many pagan temples were closed or even destroyed. Slowly the Church began to undertake missionary work beyond the frontiers of the empire. The Goth Ulfilas converted the Goths and translated the Bible; the Goths passed the new faith on to other Germanic tribes, such as the Vandals. The first tribe to become Catholic was the Franks, in about 506, soon to be followed by the Visigoths. In the fifth century the Western provinces of the empire were overrun by the barbarian Goths, Vandals, and Huns. Following the large decrease of population caused by epidemics, the Roman army had been forced to draw its recruits from the barbarian tribesmen and was itself now under barbarian generals. In the weakened empire of the fifth century, Western emperors exercised less power than generals, and the imperial succession ended when a German leader, Odoacer, decided in 476 to rule without an emperor. The end of the line of Western emperors, however, made little difference to either church or state, as in the West the position of the papacy was enhanced by the decline of state power, and this prepared the way for the popes' temporal sovereignty over parts of Italy (which they retained from the seventh to the nineteenth century).

With the barbarian invasions came the destruction of Western schools, and the churches and monasteries in particular became the repositories of Christian and philosophical writings that were created in late antiquity. The main preservers and transmitters of ancient culture were, from this time on and throughout the Middle Ages, the monks. Monasticism had begun in the Egyptian desert in the fourth century with Anthony the Hermit and with Pachomius, the first organizer of an ascetic community under a rule of obedience. The manual work of monks often was the copying of manuscripts. As the empire slowly crumbled under the pressure of barbarian invasions, the most

*The Temptation of St. Antony.* Center and inner panels of the Antony triptych. Oil on wood, by Hieronymous Bosch, c. 1450–1516. Museu Nacional de Arte Antiga, Lisbon.

ancient versions of the gospels, of the first biblical translations, as well as the writings of the first Church Fathers were preserved in the monasteries that began to appear throughout Europe at the time. Monasticism, for many centuries, was not only the cultivation of intimacy with God but also the safekeeping of ancient wisdom.

The gradual fall of the Roman Empire had a profound effect on the development of Christianity. In Europe, the land mass that had given birth to the empire, the Christian faith was developing fast, bringing comfort and hope to the people whose main culture was breaking down all around them. concerned far more with procedure, the Western Church in Europe had little time for theological speculation. The Eastern churches in North Africa and Greece, however, were less distracted by the destruction of the empire, for they mostly had developed monastic orders for whom theological speculation was paramount. The greatest controversy between the Western and Eastern churches was focused on whether faith is caused by divine

grace or human freedom. In other words, the main argument between the two churches was whether man can actively participate in his own salvation by opening his soul to receiving the grace of God. Or is God's grace bestowed only upon his chosen children, and thus entirely dependent on his will?

Few Christians today realize that there is a wide divergence between the primitive Church (of which the Eastern and Western churches formed two geographical branches) and its successor churches in the West (both Catholic and Protestant) in the understanding of how we are saved. The important differences at this juncture in history between Eastern and Western mysticism can be summarized in this way: the Western tradition is essentially the juridical/Augustinian view that human will is shackled by original sin, and so we can be saved only by unearned acts of divine grace that are ultimately pre-

destined. Augustine saw human free will as fallen and corrupt—a force in opposition to divine grace. Calvinism is perhaps its most extreme form, but this Augustinian teaching has endured in all branches of Western Christianity. Mainline Protestant theologians have only recently abandoned the Augustinian premises of original sin and atonement.

The Eastern position derives from the very different teachings of Saint Maximus the Confessor, the seventh-century Greek theologian and mystic. Along with Saint Gregory of Nyssa before him, Maximus is one of the great systematizers of the essential early Church doctrine of deification (in Greek, *theosis*). Far from being shackled by original sin, Maximus and Gregory taught that we can actively participate in our salvation, and that our free-will choices, in communion with divine grace, would one day lead to God-like perfection—deification.

Maximus's view of salvation in contrast with Augustine's is summarized below by the distinguished historian Jaroslav Pelikan in his book *The Spirit of Eastern Christendom*:

*An epitome of the contrast [with the Augustinian view of the West] is the formula of Maximus: "Our salvation finally depends on our own will." The dichotomy represented by the antithesis between Pelagianism [the rejected Latin doctrine of salvation by reliance on human will] and Augustinianism was not part of Maximum's thought. Instead, his doctrine of salvation is based on the idea of participation and of communion which excludes neither grace nor freedom, which were established once and for all in the incarnate Word and his "two wills."*

The "two wills" are the human and the divine, incarnated in Jesus, and with which all those who embark on a spiritual quest must wrestle. According to Jaroslav Pelikan "the antithesis between divine grace and freedom, which dogged Western theology for many centuries, did not present a problem in that form for Eastern Christian thought."

The Eastern Church sees salvation as a continuing process of "progression," a spiritual awakening in grace, leading eventually to our deification. The Eastern Church would centuries later consider a tragic error the simplistic evangelistic Protestant formula that salvation depends on being "born again" by virtue of the belief that "Jesus died for our sins."

In the 1960s and 1970s, the Campus Crusade for Christ led thousands of college students into the born-again brand of conversion typical of today's evangelical Christianity. In his book *Dancing Alone*, former Crusade leader and recent Orthodox convert Frank Schaeffer contrasts "born-againism" with the Orthodox experience of deification. Schaeffer was perhaps most responsible for leading the Campus Crusade for Christ into the Orthodox Church:

*The American Protestant looks for a magical instantaneous "silver bullet" solution to sin. He calls this the "born again" experience. But according to Holy Tradition, just saying that one is born again is meaningless. It does not entail the necessary. . . use of our free will to choose God's way again and again, which the historical Church taught is the only way we can become like God, to strive to become "deified"— in other words, imitate Christ and through imitation to become God-like ourselves.*

In the theology of the Eastern Church, which later came be known as the Orthodox tradition, simple conversion was seen as but a minor step toward the glorious goal, and the real purpose of human life on earth was to become God-like. As modern Russian theologian Georges Florovsky writes in *Bible, Church, Tradition: An Eastern Orthodox View*: "The ultimate aim and purpose of human life was defined in the Patristic tradition as theosis, divinization." And the venerable modern Orthodox theologian and bishop Timothy Ware states: "Such, according to the teaching of the Orthodox Church, is the final goal at which every Christian must aim: to become God, to attain *theosis*, 'deification' or 'divinization.' For Orthodoxy our salvation and redemption mean our deification."

The Church Fathers often spoke of a progression in the growth of grace: the fullness of grace was granted potentially in baptism; actual divine grace was freely received through the whole course of life by a blending of man's efforts and God's help, leading finally to perfection, union with God. Notably, this blending of human and divine will was often referred to as *synergia*, the Greek term first coined by the Patristic writer John of Damascus that was later taken up by Maximus and Gregory of Nyssa. Today we use the word *synergy* to denote two vibrations that work together in harmony—it is interesting to remember that originally the two vibrations were those of God and us.

It is easy to forget that the Orthodox doctrine of deification was biblically based. In the famous saying of Peter, Christ saved us so that *"we may become partakers of the divine nature"* (2 Peter 1:4). Orthodox theologians leaned on this and other passages in creating this teaching. (See especially John 17:22-3 and 2 Corinthians 8:9).

After centuries of development, the notion of deification reached its classical expression in the seventh century, especially in Maximus. And at the conclusion of the evolution of the Patristic tradition in the fourteenth century,

*Christus
Pantokrator,*
byzantine
mosaic, 11th
c. Hosios
Lukas Cloister,
Greece.

the doctrine of deification became—in the hands of Gregory Palamas—the
capstone of the religious anthropology of Orthodoxy. Maximus's theological
achievement culminated the line of Patristic thought that had begun as a
dialectic in the Eastern congregations at least three hundred years earlier with
Saint Athanasius, the celebrated defender of the doctrine of Incarnation at
Nicaea. Historians now point out that Athanasius's central argument to the
Council of Nicaea was the basis of the later doctrine of deification; he declared
that if Jesus is not both fully God and fully man, then we cannot logically share
in the divine nature. His famous statement about the Incarnation of God epit-
omizes the Orthodox Concept of deification: "He became man so that man
might become God."

The Western view on grace and salvation promoted primarily by Saint
Augustine was diametrically opposite: Augustine ascribed all credit to God.
The British monk Pelagius protested that Augustine was destroying responsi-
bility and denying the capacity of man to do what God commands. But the
Augustinian trend was to develop and take root in the West for many centuries.

Disbelieving the power of the human spirit to transform and become divine, the West saw human nature and thus all nature as essentially corrupt and fallen. While the Orthodox Church believed that the Fall was a divorce from one's grace and that original sin could be redeemed by constant contemplation of God, the West remained rigid in viewing the Fall as permanent. The reigning spirituality of the approaching Middle Ages was hostile to the environment and hostile to human nature: it never taught people to be compassionate toward themselves, their bodies, their enemies, or their imaginations. Scientific pursuit—the pursuit that follows the awe we feel about the workings of the universe that contains us—was considered heretical for many centuries.

The human spirit, however, is eternally hungry for divine grace, and if it was not to be cultivated from within the human heart, then it was to be worshiped on the outside—in the saints who, perhaps as a reaction, appeared in droves to keep the light aflame in the Dark Ages following the end of the Roman Empire. The saints within the Christian tradition were essentially pious individuals whom God had chosen as vessels of His divine grace on earth, at His service, doing His work among the faithful. The saints were just intermediaries between heaven and the world and thus posed no theological problems, as no saint would ever claim that his power was his own. The cult of sainthood was a powerful movement within Western Christianity, so powerful in fact that at one point it threatened to rival the worship of God. The saints were the ones who brought the grace of God—manifested as healings, miracles, and conversions of faith—down to the people. Today, the official canon of the Roman Catholic Church celebrates a different saint each day of the year. In addition to these there are several hundred more saints, many of whom are largely forgotten, and further hundreds of would-be saints waiting to be included in this list of the spiritually privileged. In order to accommodate them all there is a celebration on the first day of November, appropriately named All Saints Day, when they are all given tribute. It was in fact the issue of sainthood that began the rupture that would materialize as the split between the Roman Catholic and the Protestant churches.

In the seventh century the Eastern Empire was fighting for its life, first against the Persians and then the Arabs, and the Balkans were occupied by the Slavs. The submergence of Alexandria, Antioch, and Jerusalem—the ancient capitals of Christendom—under Muslim rule left the patriarch of Constantinople with enhanced authority, whereas the Slav invasions drove a wedge between East and West that encouraged separate religious developments. Western Church interests, on the other hand, were protected by the Frankish kings, and the papal-Frankish alliance reached its climax in the papal coronation of Charlemagne as the first Holy Roman Emperor at Rome on Christmas Day, 800. The Holy Roman Empire lasted until 1806.

The East, however, was troubled by the rise of Islam and the Arab campaign to subjugate nonbelievers by military conquest that broke upon the Byzantine Empire in 634, just as it was exhausted after defeating Persia. The will to resist was wholly absent. In 678 and again in 718, the Arabs were at the walls of Constantinople. Despite the Muslim conquests, the monasteries in the Christian East kept their mystical traditions intact, translating ancient manuscripts into Greek and other languages.

Western monks were sent on evangelical missions—there remained immense areas of Europe to which the Gospel had not yet been brought. Gregory I (the Great) evangelized the Anglo-Saxons, who in turn sent missionaries to northwestern Europe, to what is now the Netherlands, and to Hesse, Thuringia, and Bavaria. As a consequence of the Christian work in Germany, a mission to Scandinavia was initiated, and the mission reached Iceland by 996. In the tenth century the mission from Germany moved eastward to Bohemia, to the Magyars, and (from 966) to the Poles. By 1050 most of Europe was under Christian influence, with the exception of Muslim Spain.

In the Byzantine sphere, early missions went to the Hunnish tribesmen north of the Caucasus. The Nestorians, entrenched in Persia, carried the Gospel to the Turks and across central Asia to China. In the ninth century the mission to the Slavs began with the creation of a Slavonic alphabet in order to translate the Bible into the Slavonic language. Achievements such as these made possible the faith and medieval culture of both Russia and Serbia.

The mutual distrust between the Eastern and Western churches erupted again in the middle of the eleventh century after papal imposition of Latin customs upon Greeks in southern Italy. The patriarch of Constantinople closed Latin churches in Constantinople as a reprisal. Cardinal Humbert came from Italy to protest, was accorded an icy reception, and left a bull of excommunication (July 16, 1054) on the altar of the great church of Hagia Sophia. The bull condemned Michael Cerularius, the patriarch of Constantinople; the Orthodox version of the doctrine of the Holy Spirit; the marriage of Orthodox priests; and the use of leavened bread for the Eucharist. The papal bull from Rome excommunicated the Eastern Church and its fundamental practices; Constantinople, in turn, also saw fit to excommunicate the papal delegation. At the time, the breach was treated as a minor storm, but as East and West became more estranged, people looked back on the events of 1054 as marking the final breach between the Roman Catholic and Orthodox churches. Not until December 7, 1965, were the mutual excommunications of 1054 abolished, by Pope Paul VI and the ecumenical patriarch Athenagoras.

Byzantine and Latin Christianity had become increasingly isolated from each other by difference of language, culture, politics, and religious practices and followed their own course in shaping their heritage. Byzantine Christianity developed a spiritual theology based upon the contemplation of the three words most sacred to Christians: *Theos*, *Logos*, and *Spiritus*. The East understood the practice of theology only as a personal communion with *Theos*, the Father, through the *Logos*, Christ, in *Spiritus*, the Holy Spirit—an experience lived in a state of constant prayer. Consequently, the Eastern Church possessed no handbooks of "spiritual theology" as we have them today, but manuals of step-by-step instruction on prayer and contemplation. Theophane the Recluse, the greatest writer in the Russian spiritual tradition, strongly emphasized this by saying: "Let us hope that someone will collect the prayers written by the Holy Fathers, for they would make a true handbook of salvation."

The Western Church, in the meantime, was to undergo one of its most profound transformations following the end of the Roman Empire—the major centers of activity were no longer the imperial cities that had dotted the classical landscape, but small communities scattered amid clearings in the forests that had grown to cover the whole continent. Monasteries and abbeys were established, and in the high Middle Ages they sustained the local economy by renting out land to the peasants and by encouraging agriculture and crafts in the local villages. Monks and saints became fervent advocates of ascetic mysticism. Bernard de Cluny, a monk, poet, and Neoplatonic moralist, was the perfect representation of the monastic ideal of the time; he founded the great Benedictine abbey of Cluny, near Lyon in France, one of the major monastic centers of medieval Europe. His writings condemned humanity's search for earthly happiness and criticized the immorality of the times. Bernard's major work, *De contemptu mundi* ("On Condemning the World") expresses the disdain for the material world characteristic of Neoplatonism and of the style of mysticism that was developing in the West. Decrying the transitory nature of earthly life, Bernard maintained that man's satisfaction could be found only in the spiritual existence of the next world, which could be reached most directly by a rigorous asceticism. With biting satire, he also censured the moral decay of the Western Church. He concluded with a vividly apocalyptic description of heaven and hell that may have influenced Dante's *The Divine Comedy*.

Right: *Hagia Sophia*, by Gaspard Fossati, 19th c. From the Stapleton Collection.

# Chapter Four

## The Western Mystical Tradition

HE WESTERN CHURCH WAS TO ENTER MEDIEVAL HISTORY through the doors opening into the Dark Ages from the progressive decline of the Roman Empire around 600 C.E. Much of Europe, with the signs of Roman civilization lying in decay all over, was covered by a mantle of trees—an immense thick forest that extended in different belts, west to east, all the way from the Rhine across the Danube across the eastern borders of Muslim-occupied territories, and all the way north through central Europe to the Scandinavian borders with the tundra at the polar circle. Ancient Roman roads had fallen into disuse and many terminated in a barrier of trees, and Europe in the Dark Ages had become almost unknowable. In its densest areas the Hercynian German forest was said to take nine days to cross north to south. But this was a mere excursion compared to crossing west to east; according to common opinion at the time, travelers had journeyed sixty days eastward without ever seeing the edge of the forest, and this was within Germany alone! The presence of the forest changed the European way of life completely: people were assembled in small communities that were separated by vast distances of trees; economies of animals, crafts, and crops were maintained between cleared and wooded space; and the cities that had been the main urban centers of the Christian Church had fallen with the Empire. In the busy medieval society of men, agriculture, and animals, the Christian Church moved from a primarily urban mode to a countrified existence. From at least the seventh century many monasteries were established in woodlands not as retreats but to take advantage of the thriving natural economy, and left their marks on place-names such as Waldkirch (Church of the Wood) and Klosterwald (Monastery Forest). The Christian Church owned vast areas of land until well into this century, land it had begun to acquire in the high Middle Ages.

The ranks of the mystics included not only the monks and nuns in the monasteries but also the forest hermits. From Ireland to Bohemia, penitents fled from the temptations of the world into the woodland depths. In solitude they would seek mystical transports or wage war against the ordeals delivered by the demonic darkness. The indeterminate, boundless forest became Europe's version of the Biblical desert wilderness to which it was often compared: a place to test faith and where the true believer would be put to the severest trials. But it was also a site of miracles, where stags would appear bearing the holy cross, and the leprous and the lame could suddenly be cured with a root or a bough.

It was not easy to protect this holy seclusion. Once established in anchorite solitude, many hermits became so famous that they attracted throngs of pilgrims. Some hermits became charismatic preachers, like Peter the Hermit, who lived in the eleventh century and delivered powerful sermons to the congregations in the forests. Others institutionalized collective seclusion by founding monasteries of penitents, and in order to maintain solitude, they sited them atop inaccessible mountains or in the midst of marshes. The hagiographies (lives of the saints) are full of stories of sainted holy men such as Ermelande, who turned his eighth-century monastery on an island of the Loire, set in densest and darkest woods, into a virtual paradise. Medieval monasteries finally succeeded in taming the wildness, paganism, and barbarism that had plagued Christianity until then. They became centers of healing as the monks learned the medicinal properties of plants and used them in food and potions; they became centers of learning as ancient manuscripts were copied and illuminated in gold leaf after translation from Greek or Latin; they became sanctuaries for the soul, settled in the quiet and contemplative medieval world.

*The Creation-centered Mystics*

Although the predominant spiritual mode of medieval Europe was characterized by subject-object dualism, the view of nature as fallen, the view of man as intrinsically sinful, and a mysticism consisting mainly of ascetic practices intended to expurgate the flesh from its corruption, there slowly arose another tradition of spirituality in the West. Author and priest Matthew Fox names this different mystical strand "creation-centered spirituality":

> *That tradition, the creation-centered one, considers the environment itself to be a divine womb, holy, worthy of reverence and respect. We are in the divinity and the divinity is*

> *in us according to this tradition—and by "we" I do not mean merely the two-legged ones but the entire universe: atoms and galaxies, rain and whales, trees and fish, dogs and rabbits, and humans too. While little has been heard from this tradition in religious and theological circles in centuries, the fact is that this tradition was alive and well in medieval Europe for a lively period of three hundred years. This was the period that gave us Chartres Cathedral, Hildegard's amazing music and mandalas, Francis of Assisi's empassioned and Sufi-like life style, Aquinas's Summa, Mechtild of Magdeburg's journal and political involvement, Eckhart's mystical prophetic genius, the rich theology of the* Theologica

*Germanica,* and Julian of Norwich's *metaphysics of goodness.*
*The twelfth-century renaissance in Europe was in great measure*
*an awakening to the creation-centered tradition, which meant first*
*and foremost an awakening to nature itself.*
— Matthew Fox, *Wrestling with the Prophets*

In the following sections we will read and learn about the life stories and some of the key spiritual concepts that were cherished and developed by these "creation-centered" mystics. Hildegard of Bingen (1098-1179) and Meister Eckhart (c. 1260-1327) lived in the Rhineland area of Germany. This was an area where Celts had come to settle as Christians in the seventh century. The Celts were well known for their worship of and spiritual kinship with nature; their mystery schools were located inside forest groves, and their rune alphabet was based on the names and magical properties of trees. The Celts had been both feared and persecuted by the Romans, especially in the northern parts of the empire, including Britain. In the Middle Ages, many had converted to Christianity and brought to the new faith a flavor of their ancient wisdom about the natural world and the workings of the cosmos. The Celts who had become Christian, however, depended for their theology on the Eastern tradition—*theosis,* or man's ability to cultivate God within—rather than the austere and punishing Augustinian views. John the Scot, born a Celt, was for instance the first to translate Eastern Christianity's mystical works into Latin. Ancient Celtic wisdom contributed greatly to Western culture, influencing its mystics and its spiritual outlook. Author Paul Henry Lang shows a keen understanding of how ideas flowed from the pagans to inform the Christian West:

> *Ireland and Scotland had never experienced civilization as a reality. The Celts came*
> *into contact with Rome, the colonizer, much as the East Indians made the acquain-*
> *tance of modern England. Consequently they did not face the grave conflict between*

Opposite:
*Hildegard's*
*vision: The*
*Angel's Song of*
*Praise.*
Painting by
Hildegard of
Bingen, 12th c.
From the
Rupertsberger
Codex.

*ancient learning and Christian faith which caused a sharp reaction in the countries within the orbit of classical civilization. They were thus eminently suited to bring about a reconciliation of the two philosophies and outlooks on life, and communicated their ideas not only to their neighbors the Anglo-Saxons, but through their monastic settlements in the Frankish Empire and northern Italy, to the whole of Christian Europe.*

The Celtic oneness with nature also influenced the mysticism of Saint Francis of Assisi, whose *Canticle of the Creatures,* a hymn honoring and praising elements of the cosmos, is one of the most famous and best-loved prayers inherited by us today. Another feature of the creation-centered mystics was their acknowledgment of women's spiritual experience; Hildegard, Julian of Norwich and Mechtild of Magdeburg were women mystics whose contribution was neglected for many centuries and is fortunately being re-appraised today. They saw the world as whole, the role of the mystically awakened individual as repairing the rupture caused by dualism, and prayer and salvation as holism and a return to union. In this respect they were in profound contrast to Saint Augustine, whose views of nature as corrupt were to warp centuries of patriarchy and injure the environment—and from which we are recovering only today. The message of these medieval women mystics closely resonates with contemporary authors such as Susan Griffin and Mary Daly, who have called us through their books to abandon the old ways and to see the sacred that exists in our relationship with nature. Both authors have rightly pointed out that the abusive treatment of nature and of women go hand in hand, and it is a painful inheritance from the patriarchal attitudes of the medieval Church.

In the exploration of these mystics we will discern some spiritual themes that constellate their basic ecological consciousness and that Matthew Fox has listed in his book *Wrestling with the Prophets:*

1. The goodness (blessing of creation)
2. The goodness and blessing that the earth itself is (including human earthiness or bodiliness)

3. Cosmic awareness, cosmic consciousness, and a psychology of microcosm, macrocosm

4. A theology of panentheism as most properly naming our relationship to God

5. The motherhood of God and the human vocation to co-create the cosmos

6. Compassion understood as interdependence and justice making

Panentheism is defined by Matthew Fox as our relationship to God in the context of "all things in God and God in all things" or as Mechtild of Magdeburg declared, "the day of my spiritual awakening was the day I saw and knew I saw all things in God and God in all things." Panentheism is the view of all creation existing in the divine and the divine infusing all creation like a web. This all-embracing mysticism was born in the Middle Ages but speaks to us today when we are so in need of redirecting our spiritual passions toward repairing the split between us and God, between inner and outer, between male and female, between higher and lower, between good and bad—a split that is the cause of our fractured world today. These mystics can teach us, even across centuries, treasures about what is true worship and what it can accomplish when it is directed to wholeness-making. The Middle Ages was the last time when the West had a living cosmology—the merging of mysticism and the process of nature to explain the living universe—and the mystics of that era have much to teach us and offer great inspiration for us today. They all intimately understood and lived in the paradigm that we are trying to recapture— "all things in God and God in all things."

## Hildegard of Bingen (1098-1179)

*The marvels of God*
*are not brought forth*
*from one's self.*

*Rather,*
*it is more like a chord,*
*a sound that is played.*

*The tone does not come*
*out of the chord itself,*
*but rather,*
*through the touch of the musician.*

*I am, of course,*
*the lyre and the harp*
*of God's kindness.*

Hildegard of Bingen, who was born nine hundred years ago in Bavaria, was a poetess, abbess, musician, artist, healer, scientist, theologian, prophet, and mystic. Writing in Latin, a language perhaps too grammatically cumbersome to express her fluid mysticism, Hildegard speaks of wholeness, of the complex interweavings of the human, the cosmic, and the divine that merge into a deep oneness.

Hildegard lived in a convent from the time she was eight years old, and in her writings she reports that even at that young age she had knowledge of her intimacy with God. It was not until she was forty years old that she began to write down some of the visions and insights that she received throughout her life since childhood. It was through the efforts of Bernard de Clairvaux, a Cisterian monk and great mystic who called the world to devotion to the sacred feminine as represented by the Virgin Mary, that Hildegard's writings were presented to a Papal Synod in 1147, spreading her fame quickly.

She wrote several texts: the first, titled *Scivia*, contains thirty-six of her visions with commentaries on them; among her other works are a book on nature, *Liber Physicae Elementorum*; a book on health, *Liber Compositae Medicinae*; a commentary on the gospels, an exposition of Saint Benedict's rule, and a theological work on Saint Anastasius. After her writings were presented at the Synod,

*Vision of the Holy Hildegard,* illumination by Hildegard of Bingen, 12th c. From the *Liber Divinorum Operum Simplicis Hominis,* Biblioteca Governativa Statale, Lucca.

popes, abbots, emperors, peasants, mystics, and even those who had been excommunicated sought her advice and were guided by her visions and insight.

Hildegard saw herself as "showered with the gentle raindrops of divine inspiration." Hildegard brought together holiness and earthiness, and her poems show her deep bond with nature, which she saw as infused with the divine, thus radically departing from the preexistent images of the purely transcendent God. Her enlightened vision merged what we normally tend to separate: the intuitive-emotional with the rational-analytical, weaving together a spirituality that celebrates wholeness and unity. If Saint Francis of Assisi postulated a model of the universal community of creatures, Hildegard shows us the earth as a region of delight, a marriage bed between God and humanity where life is rendered rich and fertile and prayer is a celebration of fruitfulness.

> *I am the one whose praise*
> *echoes on high.*
>
> *I adorn all the earth.*
>
> *I am the breeze*
> *that nurtures all things*
> *green.*
> *I encourage blossoms to flourish with ripening fruits.*
>
> *I am led by the spirit to feed*
> *the purest streams.*
>
> *I am the rain*
> *coming from the dew*
> *that causes the grasses to laugh*
> *with the joy of life.*
>
> *I call forth tears,*

the aroma of holy work.

I am the yearning for good.

Who is the Holy Spirit?
The Holy Spirit is a Burning Spirit.
It kindles
the hearts of humankind.
Like tympanun and lyre it plays them,
gathering volume in the temple of the soul.

Holy Spirit is
Life-giving-life,
all movement.

Root of all being.

Purifier of all impurity.

Absolver of all faults.

Balm of all wounds.

Radiant life, worthy of all praise,
The Holy Spirit resurrects and awakens
everything that is.

ॐ

The blowing wind,
the mild, moist air,
the exquisite greening
of trees and grasses—

In their beginning,
in their ending,
they give God their praise.

❧

As the Creator loves his creation,
so Creation loves the Creator.

Creation,
of course,
was fashioned to be adorned,
to be showered,
to be gifted with the love of
the Creator.

The entire world has been embraced
by this kiss.

God has gifted creation with everything
that is necessary.

❧

Divinity is aimed at humanity.

❧

Like billowing clouds,
like the incessant gurgle of the brook,
the longing of the soul can never be
stilled.

It is this longing with which holy
persons seek their work from God.

## Francis of Assisi (1181-1226)

*Lord, make me an instrument of thy peace.*
*Where there is hatred, let me sow love;*
*Where there is injury, parson;*
*Where there is doubt, faith;*
*Where there is despair, hope;*
*Where there is darkness, light;*
*Where there is sadness, joy:*
*Divine Master, grant that I may not so much seek*
*To be consoled as to console,*
*To be understood as to understand,*
*To be loved as to love;*
*For it is in giving that we receive;*
*It is in pardoning that we are pardoned;*
*It is in dying to self that we are born to eternal life.*

Francesco Bernardone was born in Assisi, in the province of
Perugia, in central Italy, in 1181. He was the son of a wealthy
merchant draper, and as a youth he led a frivolous and care-
free life that ended abruptly when he was recruited to go to
war. He was wounded in battle and returned home very ill;
while recovering, he experienced an urgent call to bring a
deeper dimension of religiousness into the world. One day,
while praying in the church of San Damiano, he heard the statue
of Christ speak to him, urging him, "Francesco, repair my falling
house." He took the words literally, and without any thought or asking
for permission, he sold a great quantity of his father's goods in order to pay for
the repairs needed for the church. His father, angry at what he considered
Francesco's youthful foolishness, disinherited and disowned him. Francesco left
home to wed "Lady Poverty," and many of his once reckless friends joined him.
Together they lived in poverty, chastity, and faith in God. Three years later, in

1210, Pope Innocent III authorized Francesco and eleven companions to be wandering preachers of Christ. The headquarters of the brothers was the Porziuncola chapel at Santa Maria degli Angeli, on the outskirts of Assisi. The brothers traveled throughout Italy, calling people to simplicity and repentance. In 1212 Francesco founded with Claire (who was canonized Saint Claire of Assisi in 1255) the neighboring community of the Poor Ladies.

By 1217 the movement of the followers of Francesco was beginning to take the shape of a monastic order. So many members had joined that it became necessary to set up communities elsewhere in Italy, and some monks traveled to other parts of Europe. In 1221 Cardinal Ugolino, a friend of Francesco, revised the rule of the order, reiterating the vows of poverty, humility, and evangelical freedom that had characterized its founder. In 1224, while Francesco was praying on Monte la Verna in the Apennines, stigmata—bleeding scars corresponding to the five wounds inflicted on Jesus on the cross—appeared on his body. The stigmata never left him, and he suffered intensely until he joined "Sister Death" in 1226.

Saint Francis of Assisi remains to this day one of the most loved and most popular saints of Christianity, representing simplicity, directness, and a model of single-mindedness for many. He was not just an inspired mystic and individualist—his tremendous power and insight made him one of the best representatives of the qualities of Christ. In 1979 Pope John Paul II proclaimed him patron saint of the ecological movement on account of Saint Francis's deep affinity with the natural world. His songs honoring Sister Moon, Brother Sun, Sister Water, and Brother Wolf are still sung by Italian children today.

*The Canticle of the Creatures*

Saint Francis composed this beautiful song when he was gravely ill and close to death in Assisi. Friar Bonaventura, the most literate of Saint Francis's monks, explained the saint's affinity with nature as a complete merging with the universe that surrounded him: "For by the impulse of this unexampled devotion he tasted that fountain of goodness that streams forth, as in rivulets, in every created thing, and he perceived as it were a heavenly harmony in the concord of

View of Assisi with Church and Cloister of San Francesco. The town of Subiaso is just visible in the background. Photo taken in 1982.

properties and actions granted to them by God, and sweetly exhorted them to praise the Lord." Legend tells that when a quarrel broke out between the mayor and bishop of Assisi, Francis added a strophe on forgiveness, and they became reconciled when the Franciscan brothers sang the canticle to them.

> *Most high, all-powerful, good Lord,*
> *all praise be yours, all glory, all honor*
> *and all blessing.*
> *To you alone, Most High, do they belong.*
> *No mortal lips are worthy*
> *to pronounce your name.*
>
> *All praise be yours, my Lord,*
> *in all your creatures,*
> *especially Sir Brother Sun*
> *who brings the day;*
> *and light you give us through him.*

*The Stigmatisation of the Holy Franciscus*, oil on wood by Giotto di Bondone, c. 1295–1300. Musee du Louvre, Paris.

*How beautiful he is, how radiant in his splendor!*
*Of you, Most High, he is the token.*

*All praise be yours, my Lord,*
*for Brother Wind and the Air,*
*and fair and stormy*
*and every kind of weather*
*by which you nourish everything*
*you have made.*

*All praise be yours, my Lord,*
*for Sister Water;*
*she is so useful and lowly,*
*so precious and pure.*

*All praise be yours, my Lord,*
*for Brother Fire*
*by whom you brighten the night.*
*How beautiful he is,*
*how gay, robust and strong!*

*All praise be yours, my Lord,*
*for Sister Earth, our mother*
*who feeds us, rules us*
*and produces all sorts of fruit*
*and colored flowers and herbs.*

*All praise be yours, my Lord,*
*for those who forgive one another*
*for love of you*
*and endure infirmity and tribulation.*
*Happy are they who endure these in peace*

for by you, Most High, they will be crowned.

All praise be yours, my Lord,
for our Sister Physical Death
from whose embrace no mortal can escape.
Woe to those who die in mortal sin!
Happy are those she finds
doing your most holy will!
The second death can do no harm to them.

Praise and bless my Lord
and give him thanks and serve him
with great humility.


Dear Brother Fire

My Brother Fire,
outdoing all created things in splendor,
the Most High created you
mighty, fair and useful.
Be kind to me at this hour,
be courteous,
for I have long loved you in the Lord.
I pray the great Lord
who created you
to temper your heat now
so that, burning me gently,
I may be able to bear it.

The Praises of the Virtues

Hail, Queen Wisdom!
The Lord keep you with your sister,
pure, holy Simplicity.
Lady Holy Poverty,
the Lord keep you with your sister,
holy Humility.
Lady Holy Love,
the Lord keep you with your sister,
holy obedience.
All you holy virtues,
the Lord protect you,
from whom you proceed.
No one on earth can possess any one of you
unless he first dies to self.
Whoever possesses one
without offending against the others
possesses all.
Whoever offends against one
possesses none
and offends against all.
Each one and every one of you
banishes vice and sin.
Holy Wisdom
confounds Satan and all his wiles.
Pure, holy Simplicity
confounds all the wisdom of this world.
Holy Poverty
confounds all greed, the great ones
of this world and all that it is in this world.
Holy Love
confounds all the temptations

*of the flesh and the devil*
*and all human fears.*
*Holy obedience*
*confounds all selfish desires,*
*mortifies our lower nature*
*and makes our body ready*
*to obey the Spirit and our fellow beings,*
*making us submissive to men*
*but even to wild animals*
*in so far as the Lord permits.*

*May the burning and tender might*
*of your love,*
*I beseech you, O Lord,*
*ravish my soul*
*from all earthly things:*
*so that I may die*
*for love of my love.*

Mechtild of Magdeburg (1210-1280)

*See there within the flesh*
*Like a bright wick, englazed*
*The soul God's finger lit*
*To give her liberty,*
*And joy and power and love,*
*To make her crystal, like*
*As maybe, to Himself.*

Mechtild was born into a wealthy German family in 1210. She was educated but did not learn Latin, and she is one of the first European mystics to have written ecstatic poetry in the vernacular—a rich German dialect that gave her spiritual images a concrete and substantial tone. When she was just twelve, she received what she called her first "greeting from God," when she saw "all things in God and God in all things." The visitation from God was so powerful that it would shape her life, because this experience was repeated every day since.

*The true greeting from God, which comes from the heavenly flood out of the spring of the flowing Trinity, has such power that it takes all strength from the body and lays the soul bare to itself. Thus it sees itself as one of the blessed and receives in itself divine glory.*

Mechtild was probably twenty-three when she felt compelled to leave her family and friends and travel to Magdeburg, Germany, and affiliated herself with one of the most extraordinary movements in European history—the Beguines. The Beguines were "an order that was not an order" of women who led strict religious lives but never adopted a rule. Some lived with their families, while others formed communal households. They had no saintly founder; they asked for no authorization from Rome; they never organized or sought any patrons. It was a spontaneous movement characterized by an open structure that was highly unusual at the time. The first Beguines started in Liège, in what is now Belgium, around 1210, and very quickly established communities in Germany and France. In the fourteenth century, the great Beguinage at Ghent was surrounded with walls and moats; inside were two churches,

*Madonna im Ahrenkleid. Oil and tempera on wood by the Sterzinger Meister, c. 1450. Church of Sterzing, Germany.*

eighteen convents, more than a hundred houses, a brewery, and an infirmary. Magdeburg, a good-sized town, also had a Beguine house and was residence to friars of the Dominican order. One of them, Heirich Halle, who became Mechtild's confessor, had been a student of Albert the Great, under whom Thomas Aquinas had studied also.

Mechtild did not start writing about her spiritual experiences until 1250, when their sheer intensity made her feel she could no longer keep silent. Heinrich Halle encouraged her to write, and it was he who later collected Mechtild's loose sheets into a book, *The Flowing Light of the Godhead*, and circulated it among small circles. The unembarrassed physicality and the sexual element in her words would have been understood equivocally at the time and she formed as many friends as enemies through her writing. Mechtild was never canonized, nor was her book regarded as one of the treasured mystical writings. Perhaps it was because the Church was to remain hostile to women for many centuries; perhaps it was because she belonged to the Beguines, whose way of life was to be permanently forbidden at the Council of Vienna in 1312, since they obeyed neither husbands nor priests, and they were declared to be "too free." Certain individuals recommended that her book should be burned. Mechtild was too spontaneous for medieval Europe, her love of God too unbridled. Men of letters were baffled and confused by her warmth, intensity of feeling, and use of overt sexual metaphors to describe the movement of the soul reaching out for God like a lover for her bridegroom. *The Flowing Light of the Godhead* passed into oblivion soon after the fourteenth century, did not reappear until 1860, and was not translated into English until 1953.

Mechtild used the expressions, metaphors, and movements of the language of courtly love, a poetic form that took Europe by storm a century before her birth and became the favorite style of an entire literary movement that also embraced spiritual writers. Some of her pieces are orchestrated around the dialogue leading to the seduction of the soul by God:

*[R]acing like a hunted deer*
*to the spring which is Myself.*

*She comes soaring like an eagle*
*Swinging herself from the depths*
*Up into the heights.*

God is the spring that will quench the thirsty deer, Mechtild's
metaphor for the soul. The soul brings to the Lord her treasure:

*[G]reater than the mountains,*
*Wider than the world,*
*Deeper than the sea,*
*Higher than the clouds,*
*More glorious than the sun,*
*More manifold than the stars,*
*It outweighs the whole earth!*
. . . . . . . . . . . . . .
*Lord! It is called my heart's desire!*
*I have withdrawn it from the world,*
*Denied to myself and all creatures,*
*Now I can bear it no longer.*
*Where, O Lord, shall I lay it?*
. . . . . . . . . . . . . . . .
*Thy heart's desire shall though lay somewhere*
*But in mine own Divine Heart*
*And on My human breast*
*And there alone wilt thou find comfort*
*And be embraced by My spirit.*

The Lord has declared that her desire should be placed upon His
breast. A period of preparation ensues before the embrace with the divine, a
time when the soul awaits union with the beloved that will take place in "the
shade of a brook, the resting place of love, where thou may cool thyself." The

soul sends her handmaidens away—a metaphor for transcending the senses—but they protest, pleading with her, "If you go there, then we will be blinded, for the divinity is fiery and hot. . . . Who can remain there for even one hour?" But in the poem Mechtild's soul replies:

> *Fish cannot drown in water*
> *Birds cannot sink in air,*
> *Gold cannot perish*
> *In the refiner's fire.*
> *This has God given to all creatures,*
> *To foster and seek their own nature,*
> *How then can I withstand mine?*

The soul now goes to the secret place, the innermost chamber of love, where she will meet her beloved. But God gives another trial, and tells her "Thy self must go"—the last remnants of personality, of ego, must be shed before the final embrace. The soul, frightened, worries that nothing will be left of her, and God reassures her that the only thing that will be left will be her longing and desire, which He will fill and flood with his love. The soul drops all outer garments and remains naked before her Lord:

> *Lord, now am I a naked soul*
> *And thou a God most Glorious!*
> *Our two-fold intercourse is Love Eternal*
> *Which can never die.*
> . . . . . . . . . . . . . . . . . . .
> *When two lovers secretly come together,*
> *They must often part, without parting.*

In the last two enigmatic lines of the poem Mechtild makes reference to *epectasis*, the teaching

*The Mystic Flower*, painting by Gustave Moreau, 19th c. Musee Gustave Moreau, Paris.

that the depth of God is inexhaustible—once the union is found the parting can never be permanent—a doctrine central to much of medieval mysticism.

Mechtild also uses metaphors that are almost Sufi-like—the ecstatic mystical current of Islam—to describe the intensity of her longing for God. In the following poem we are reminded of some of the symbols also used by Rumi in his *Tavern of Ruin*, when one, drunk with God, abandons oneself utterly to the embrace of the beloved, leaving all worldly cares behind:

*Wouldst thou come with me to the wine cellar?*
*That will cost thee much;*
*Even hadst thou a thousand marks*
*It were all spent in an hour!*
*If thou wouldst drink the unmingled wine*
*Thou must ever spend more than thou hast,*
*and the host will never fill thy glass to the brim!*
*Thou will become poor and naked,*
*Despised of all who would rather see themselves*
*In the dust, than squander their all in the wine cellar.*
*This also thou must suffer,*
*That thy friends look askance at thee*
*Who go with thee to the Inn.*
*How greatly they will scorn thee*
*When they cannot dare such costs*
*But must have water mixed with wine.*

Mechtild composed a poem in which she writes about the body as being the sacred chamber in which we meet God and calls us not to disdain it but to respect it, challenging the view of the time that regarded the body as corrupt and in need of punishing ascetic practices to rid it of its original sin:

*Do not disdain your body. For the soul is just as safe in*

*its body as in the kingdom of heaven—though not so certain.*
*It is just as daring—but not so strong.*
*Just as powerful—but not so constant.*
*Just as loving—but not so joyful.*
*Just as gentle—but not so rich.*
*Just as holy—but not yet so sinless.*
*Just as content—but not so complete.*

In this last selection of her book Mechtild presents us with a very powerful and moving image of the intimate dialogue between God and the soul—God calls the soul, a call sent out long ago that echoes through the universe and bounces off barriers of time and space until a crack in our being opens and the call is heard. God in search of man, man in search of God:

*God Speaks to the Soul*

*And God said to the soul:*
*I desired you before the world began.*
*I desire you now*
*As you desire me.*
*And where the desires of two come together*
*There love is perfected.*

*Thomas of Aquinas,* painting by Justus van Gent, *c.* 1476. Musee du Louvre, Paris.

*How the Soul Speaks to God*
*Lord, you are my lover,*
*My longing,*
*My flowing stream,*
*My sun,*
*And I am your reflection.*

*How God Answers the Soul*
*It is my nature that makes me love you often,*
*For I am love itself.*
*It is my longing that makes me love you intensely,*
*For I yearn to be loved from the heart.*
*It is my eternity that makes me love you long,*
*For I have no end.*

In 1270, aging and ill, Mechtild was welcomed at the Benedictine convent at Helfta, near Eisleben in Saxony, under the direction of Abbess Gertrude of Hackeborn, who trained daughters of the nobility and made the convent into a great center of learning. Shortly before her death in 1280 and after she had gone blind, Mechtild dictated her last poetry to a scribe in Helfta.

*Thomas Aquinas (1225–1323)*

*Three things are necessary for the salvation of man: to know what he ought to believe; to know what he ought to desire; and to know what he ought to do.*

Thomas was born in Roccasecca, near Aquino, in 1225. He was one of the many children of Landulf of Aquino, a nobleman of Lombard descent. Thomas was educated by the Benedictines at Monte Cassino and in Naples, where in 1244 he joined the order. His family was so shocked at the news that

he intended to become a mendicant friar that his brothers kidnapped him and locked him in a tower for a year. However, Thomas did not change his mind, and the family finally released him. He subsequently went to study under Albert the Great in Paris and Cologne, and in 1256 he completed his degree in theology. The rest of Thomas's life was devoted to teaching and to writing. At the end of 1273 he left his great work, the *Summa Theologica*, which has been translated from Latin into twenty-two volumes, unfinished, declaring that, "All I have written seems to me like so much straw compared with what I have seen and with what has been revealed to me." He was asked to attend an ecclesiastical council at Lyons, but he was ill when he undertook the journey, and died at the abbey of Fossanuova in 1323. The *Summa Theologica* earned him the name of "universal teacher"; the text is a systematic exposition of theology and has been studied since his time as a classic of enlightened thought. His influence on the Church and religious thought has been enormous. In 1567 he was declared a doctor of the Church by Pope Pius V.

*Tomistic Metaphysics*

Thomas Aquinas was a special kind of mystic; he spent hours in prayer and was graced with deep mystical insights, but he was also a scholar whose commitment was to passing on what he had "seen" to others. His main effort was to create in his *Summa Theologica* a systematic substructure for the Christian message by using Aristotelian metaphysics and dialectic. The central problem of both mysticism and Greek philosophy is the paradox of *the one and the many*. How do we, in other words, reconcile the experience of unity and multiplicity? In the ordinary state of consciousness, we see reality fragmented in many parts: trees, animals, objects, friends, family, problems, joys, worries, and so on. In the mystical, inspired state of consciousness experienced by poets, philosophers, artists, and ordinary people in extraordinary moments, reality in all its components is experienced as oneness. Another problem is the reconciliation of opposites: life and death, heaven and hell, all and nothing, etc. And the third problem, ancillary to the first two, is God to whom we pray but also in whom we live, in such a way that we are one with God and not one with God.

Thomas Aquinas resolves this conflict, which resides at the root of the meaning of life, with his theory of essence and existence. All things are by their reason of existence; all things are different by reason of their essence. When we look out into the world and see only existence, we become aware of unity. If, on the other hand, we look out into the world and see essence, then we become aware of multiplicity. In God, however, essence and existence, are one and the same thing. God is being and all beings are God; God is life and all elements of life are God. This may seem highly speculative, but many mystics have referred to Tomistic metaphysics to map out a path to realization: if we eschew all essences and concentrate on existence we gradually train our consciousness to embrace unity and abandon fragmentation, and in so doing we repair both the inner and the outer worlds by leading them to wholeness.

*Connaturality*

In his *Summa Theologica*, Thomas Aquinas speaks of two kinds of knowledge—the knowledge derived from scientific inquiry or perfect use of reason and the knowledge derived from what he calls "connaturality," from the experience of "co-naturing," being in "co-presence" with an object, penetrating its essence intimately so that the object becomes embodied in oneself. We can test these two kinds of knowledge in our own lives. There are certain things we "know" because our knowledge of them is derived from direct experience—we are united with certain experiences, have lived them, loved them, and so we "know" in an intuitive and nevertheless reliable way. Other things we know because our knowledge is derived from a logical mental process, so our knowledge is a matter of judgment, an inquiry of reason.

In the experience of connaturality one undergoes a subtle but powerful alteration of perception: in *knowing* an object the mind does not need to think of knowledge and so becomes completely still or absent, a state Zen Buddhism calls "no-mind." Be still and know—this is the true meaning of connaturality. The highest wisdom comes to us when we experience connaturality with God, when we are still and God is there. This goes beyond conceptual knowledge. It is more a being-breathing-absenting that occurs when we receive the gift of God's love. And God calls, after all, when we are empty and silent and there are no barriers to His penetration of our being. This is a mystery to be experienced and felt rather than to be reasoned. And it is on this theological ground that Thomas Aquinas's greatest force as a mystic and enlightened scholar comes to the fore. God is known as mystery: "In this life we cannot know what he is and thus we are united to him as to one unknown."

The great gift this Italian mystic left for posterity is in his ability to convey in theological terms the mystical experience: mystics fall in love with the one whom they don't know. This is the obscure night and the light of the dawn of consciousness.

## Meister Eckhart (c. 1260-c. 1327)

> *Only he to whom God is present in everything and who employs his reason*
> *in the highest degree and has enjoyment in it knows anything of true peace*
> *and has a real kingdom of heaven.*

One of the most influential mystical writers to emerge from the Rhineland area, along with Mechtild of Magdeburg, is the Dominican friar Meister Eckhart, whose charismatic ideas spread to the Netherlands and to other parts of Europe. This was an effervescent time for the continent: it enjoyed relative peace and the churches were united, everyone spoke Latin, and liturgical celebration was similar throughout the continent. At the heart of the mystical movement and the propagation of mystical writings were the Dominicans, who held fast to Thomas Aquinas.

Johannes Eckhart was born around 1260 at Hochheim. He entered the Dominican order when he was fifteen and studied in Cologne, perhaps under the Scholastic philosopher Albert the Great. The intellectual background of European universities was greatly influenced by Thomas Aquinas, who had just died. In his mid-thirties Eckhart was nominated vicar (the chief Dominican official) of Thuringia. Before and after this assignment he taught theology at Saint-Jacques's priory in Paris. It was also in Paris that he received his master's degree (1302); thereafter he was called Meister Eckhart.

*St. Dominicus burning the Albigensian Scriptures,* painting on wood by Pedro Berruguete, c. 1480-1490. Museo del Prado, Madrid.

Eckhart wrote four works in German (usually called "treatises"). At about the age of forty he wrote the *Talks of Instruction* on self-denial, the nobility of will and intellect, and obedience to God. In 1303 he became provincial (leader) of the Dominicans in Saxony and, three years later, vicar of Bohemia. His main activity, especially from 1314 on, was preaching to the contemplative nuns—the Beguines to whom Mechtild of Magdeburg had belonged, who were established throughout the Rhine River valley. He resided in Strasbourg as a prior.

The best-attested German work of this middle part of his life is the *Book of Divine Consolation,* dedicated to the queen of Hungary. His other two treatises are *The Nobleman* and *On Detachment.* The teachings of the mature

Eckhart describe four stages of the union between the soul and God: dissimilarity, similarity, identity, breakthrough. At the outset, God is all, the creature is nothing; at the ultimate stage, "the soul is above God." The driving power of this process is detachment.

Eckhart enjoyed much respect among scholars, and in his sixtieth year he was called to a professorship at Cologne. Heinrich von Virneburg—a Franciscan, and highly unfavorable to Dominicans—was the archbishop there, and it was before his court that the now immensely popular Meister Eckhart was first formally charged with heresy. To a list of errors, he replied by publishing a defense in Latin and then asked to be transferred to the pope's court in Avignon. When ordered to justify a new series of propositions drawn from his writings, he declared: "I may err but I am not a heretic, for the first has to do with the mind and the second with the will!" Before judges who had no comparable mystical experience of their own, Eckhart referred to his inner certainty: "What I have taught is the naked truth." The bull of Pope John XXII, dated March 27, 1329, condemns twenty-eight propositions extracted from the two lists. Since it speaks of Meister Eckhart as already dead, it is inferred that Eckhart died some time before, perhaps in 1327 or 1328. It also says that Eckhart had retracted the errors as charged.

Eckhart was condemned because he was a mystic speaking in poetical terms about theology—not as a scientific pursuit but as a living experience—something the Church bureaucrats could not appreciate since they lacked the common experience of it. Eckhart is like a Galileo among the mystics, proposing themes that were similar to the language and experience of Zen Buddhism. His writings resonate intimately with our modern needs, and today his views are being reevaluated and quoted as coming from a spokesman of modern spirituality. It is to be hoped that the question of Meister Eckhart will be ecclesiastically reexamined and that he will be reinstated as an orthodox voice for his mystical understanding of the Gospel of Jesus.

*When I dwelt in the ground,*
*in the bottom, in the stream, and*

*in the Source of the Godhead,*
*No one asked me where I was going or*
*what I was doing.*
*Back in the womb from which I came,*
*I had no God*
*and merely was myself.*
*. . .*

*Now the moment I flowed out from the Creator*
*all creatures stood up and shouted:*
*"Behold, here is God."*
*They were correct.*
*For you ask me: Who is God? What is God?*
*I reply: Isness.*
*Isness is God.*
*Where there is isness, there God is.*
*Creation is the giving of isness from God.*
*And that is why*
*God becomes*
*where any creature expresses God.*

*Isness is so noble. No creature is so tiny that*
*it lacks isness.*
*If a caterpillar falls off a tree,*
*it climbs up a wall*
*in order to preserve its isness.*
*So noble is isness!*
*If you were able to deprive God of isness,*
*a stone would be more noble than God, for a stone has isness.*
*What is God?*
*God is!*
*God's being is my being*
*and God's primordial being*

is my primordial being.
Wherever I am,
there is God.
The eye with which I see God
is the same eye with which God sees me.

This I know.
That the only way to live
is like the rose
which lives
without a why.

If the only prayer
you say in your entire life
is "Thank You,"
that would suffice.

Do you want to know
what goes on in the core of the Trinity?
I will tell you.
In the core of the Trinity
the Father laughs
and gives birth to the Son.
The Son laughs back at the Father
and gives birth to the Spirit.
The whole Trinity laughs
and gives birth to us.

And remember this:
All suffering comes to an end.

*The Crowning of the Holy Maria,* emaille from Limoges, France, c. 1340. Musee du Louvre, Paris.

*I once had a dream.*
*I dreamt that I, even though a man, was pregnant,*
*pregnant and full with Nothingness like a woman who*
*is with child.*
*And out of this Nothingness*
*God was born.*

*We are all meant*
*to be mothers of God.*

*Julian of Norwich* (1342-c.1415)

*All shall be well, and every kind of thing shall be well.*

Julian of Norwich was an anchoress, a recluse whose calling demanded a more extreme withdrawal from the world than even the cloistered nuns of her time had undertaken. The word *anchoress* is a cognate of a Greek word that means "to retire." In early Christianity, anchorites withdrew to the desert for the sake

of undistracted prayer and meditation. By Julian's time the withdrawal of anchorites and anchoresses was not as extreme; they remained in towns and villages, enclosed in cells that were built right up against the walls of churches. The ceremony of enclosure marked a complete departure from the world, and was in effect a kind of burial. Extreme unction was given, and the anchorite was literally sealed in, obliged under the threat of excommunication to remain there until death. Through a window she could watch and hear church services; through another that opened to the world, she could give spiritual counsel, which she was obliged to do under her oath. The purpose of anchoritic enclosure was to remain open to prayer and intimacy with God all the time, without any distractions. The rules for anchoresses during the Middle Ages were such that Julian would have had her own set of rooms and possibly her own oratory; she would also have had a maid to cook and clean for her, and perhaps a cat to catch mice. She would have been permitted to walk in the churchyard or garden for a period every day. This highly unusual set of circumstances, almost like those of an Indian sadhu in a cave, permitted Julian to reach a depth of intimacy with God that would have been impossible had she been in a busy medieval nunnery.

Julian, a contemporary of Chaucer, was the first woman to write a book in English. She gave it no title, but it has come down to us as *A Book of Showings to the Anchoress Julian of Norwich*. The "showings" were mystical messages that were literally *shown* to her by God over a period of slightly more than twenty-four hours in May 1373, when she was thirty years old. Julian wrote two versions of the book: the first was written shortly after her powerful mystical experiences and it records the "showings." The second draft was written twenty years later, and it contains large blocks of new material interposed amid the original manuscript, for apparently over the twenty years following her mystical experience she had received continuous "inward instruction." "Freely and often" God would bring the whole revelation, from beginning to end, before the "eyes of her understanding," initiating her little by little into full depth of meaning of her experiences.

Over the two decades following her experiences, Julian of Norwich matured, and was helped to become not only a visionary of great power but also a profound spiritual teacher whose themes, if considered outrageous at the time, are extremely modern and appeal to us today. In the first draft of her writings, she prefaced the text with the disclaimer "God forbid that you should say or assume that I am a teacher, for that is not and never was my intention; for I am woman, ignorant, weak and frail." Twenty years later Julian deleted this preface, for by then she knew that her power lay in her spiritual depth and in her ability to impart counsel and comfort to others. Julian was a visionary, not a scholar, and even though her prose is extremely clear and well set out, visionary writing by women was slow to be accepted by male medieval scholars, who shunned its emotional intensity, imaginative flights, and erotic imagery. But it is these very qualities that have made her writings so popular today.

The visions Julian was shown revolve around the illumination of a single soul and the subsequent testings of that soul's capacity to cling to the divine, even against the powers of hell. The visions were as vivid and as involving as any event in Julian's real physical life, for in addition to "seeings," she also received "touchings." In the vision she saw the "motherhood of God," a theme dear to many of us today who see the universe as a womb in which we are all contained:

> I saw that he is to us everything that is good and comforting for our help. He is our clothing, who wraps and enfolds us for love, embraces us and shelters us, surrounds us for his love, which is so tender that he may never desert us.
>
> . . . . . . . . . . . . . . . . . . . . . . . . . . . . . . . . . . . . . . . . . . .
>
> And in this he showed me something small, no bigger than a hazelnut, lying in the palm of my hand, . . . as round as a ball. I looked at it with the eye of my understanding and thought: What can this be? I was amazed that it could last, for I

The Ascension of
Mary, fresco
by Moraca,
16th c.

*thought that because of its littleness it would suddenly have fallen into nothing. And
I answered in my understanding: It lasts and always will, because God loves it; and
thus everything has being through the love of God.*

Is this little ball what the astronauts saw when they looked at our earth
from their spaceship? Did they see, as Julian and other mystics had seen, and
as we are awakening to see in our own lives, that the love of God infuses everything with being? The vision is delightful, and reading it today brings about a
moment of enlightenment in the reader, thinking of a nun walled up in her cell
being shown the world in the palm of her hand by a God of love.

*Our Mother in nature, our Mother in grace, because he wanted altogether to become
our Mother in all things, made the foundation of his work most humbly and most
mildly in the maiden's womb. . . .The mother's service is nearest, readiest and surest;
nearest because it is most natural, readiest because it is most loving, and surest because*

*it is truest. No one ever might or could perform this office fully, except only for him.*

. . . . . . . . . . . . . . . . . . . . . . . . . . . . . . . . . . . . . . . . . . .

*The mother can lay her child tenderly to her breast through his sweet open side, and show us there a part of the godhead and of the joys of heaven, with inner certainty of endless bliss. . . .*

*This fair, lovely word "mother" is so sweet and so kind in itself that it cannot truly be said of anyone or to anyone except of him who is the true Mother of life and of all things.*

Julian's vision also reviews the matter of sin and corruption, for, she asks, how can it be that if God has made everything as perfect as we need it, there is such a great measure of sin and guilt in the world? God reminds her, "What is impossible to you is not impossible to me." She is shown that God is never angry with us, but that we feel so guilty in His eyes that we think we are exiled from Him. This is the first step that leads us to prayer and meditation, the silence in which we find God again. If we remain in prayer and meditation, we see that God is never far away, but always there within our heart:

*When we see ourselves so foul, then we believe that God may be angry with us because of our sin. Then we are moved by the Holy Spirit through contrition to prayer, and we desire with all our might an amendment of ourselves to appease God's anger, until the time we find rest of soul and ease of conscience. And then we hope that God has forgiven us our sin: and this is true.*

Julian of Norwich shows a wonderful dance between the creature and the creator moving toward each other, coming together in suffering and uniting in what she calls "love-longing." The unresolved difficulties of life are exactly the steps that form this dance, part human, part divine:

*During our lifetime here, we have in us a marvelous mixture of both well-being and woe. We have in us our risen Lord Jesus Christ, and we have in us the wretchedness and the harm of Adam's falling. Dying, we are constantly protected by Christ. . . so afflicted in our feelings by Adam's falling. . . .And now we are raised to the one, and now we are permitted to fall to the other.*

# Chapter Five

## *The Eastern Mystical Tradition*

HE EASTERN CHURCH, WHICH EVOLVED developed from the communities set up by Jesus' disciples and from its major center in Alexandria of Egypt in the second century, spread far and wide throughout Egypt, Ethiopia, Syria, Greece, Armenia, and all the way north to Georgia and Russia. While the West developed Scholasticism and a rational theology, the East never strayed from mystical theology, because mysticism was regarded as the source and center of all knowledge. Authentic theology, according to the Byzantine Church Fathers, comes out of prayer and, above all, out of mystical prayer.

Mystical prayer in the East was Practiced in the monasteries of the desert, and Orthodox mysticism was greatly influenced by and developed from the fullness of the "desert spirituality" tradition. The earliest Christian monastic communities were founded in the deserts of Egypt. The tradition of the Desert Fathers is best represented by the hermit Saint Anthony of Egypt (c. 250–c.355), who organized his followers into primitive monastic communities early in the fourth century. These Egyptian monks and holy women led lives of extreme asceticism, renouncing family ties, sexual relations, and possessions and practicing continual prayer. Desert spirituality had a long-established practice within Judaism—the Covenant was forged in the wilderness of Sinai, many of the Old Testament prophets had received their visions in the desert, and John the Baptist and Jesus themselves retired to the wilderness outside Jerusalem to purge their souls of all evil before beginning their ministry. Following the example of Jesus' life of poverty, service, and self-denial, the early monks devoted themselves to vows of austerity, prayer, and work. Believers who chose to go into the desert as hermits were said to be answering the call of Christ: *"Jesus said to him, 'If you would be perfect, go, sell what you possess and give to the poor, and you will have treasure in heaven; and come, follow me' "* (Matthew 19:21). Monasticism spread quickly throughout the Byzantine

Empire in the fourth through the seventh centuries and was established in Kiev in 1050 and in Moscow by 1354.

The Desert Fathers inspired the Church's leading theologians, from Athanasius in the fourth century to Gregory Palamas a thousand years later, and they were the supreme model for the mystical practice of the greatest Byzantine monks from John Climacus to Gregory of Sinai. The mystical writings emanating from Mount Athos—the greatest center of Orthodox monasticism— always hearkened back to the Egyptian desert. And the later inclusion of desert texts in *The Philokalia*— the big five volumes of the teachings of the Fathers of the Church—ensured the reappearance of desert spirituality on Russian soil, contributing in no small part to the revival of Russian spirituality in the nineteenth century that is so evident in works such as Dostoyevsky's *The Brothers Karamazov*.

*Hesychia*

The deep mystical experience of these men and women in the desert, which became the kernel of Orthodox mysticism, is one that speaks powerfully to the modern world: hesychasm. This is the quiet prayer in which one recites the name of Jesus with faith and love. The word itself comes from *hesychia*, literally meaning "quiet." Hesychasm is a method that induces an altered state of consciousness similar to that produced by the recitation of mantras in Buddhism or Hinduism, in which the mind is stilled and the whole energy of body, mind, and spirit is focused toward deepening the intimacy with God. This practice demands absolute concentration, and the desert was and still is the perfect setting for achieving such a sharp and deep degree of mindfulness. With no distractions to engage our attention, just an empty landscape as the perfect

147

*Pfingsten*,
emaille by
Nicholas of
Verdun,
c. 1181.
Stiftskirche,
Klosterneuburg,
Austria.

canvas for the beginning of this powerful meditation, the geographical emptiness emulates the inner void that is the first step toward attaining hesychasm. This is the preparatory ground for beginning to align mind, body, and spirit into the single pursuit of God. Hesychasm is so absolutely engaging that it requires total attention, and years may pass before a perfect alignment can be established of all energies into one stream flowing from the individual to God. This is particularly challenging for the modern mind, so accustomed to jumping from one thing to the next within milliseconds and unable to contemplate only one object for long periods of time in emptiness and silence. Many people today, in search of the stillness that is so elusive in our own modern lives, engage in retreats in monasteries in the desert where hesychasm is still practiced. The hesychast practices of the desert mystics provided the method for carrying out the biblical injunction of "unceasing prayer," which Saint Paul urged for all believers. Bishop Kallistos Ware, lecturer in Eastern Orthodox studies at Oxford University, summarizes the practices of hesychasm:

> A hesychast in one who pursues hesychia, inner stillness or silence of the heart, in particular through the use of the Jesus Prayer. This is a short invocation, constantly repeated, usually in the form, "Lord Jesus Christ, Son of God, have mercy on me." Through inner attentiveness and the repetition of this prayer, sometimes accompanied by a physical technique involving the control of breathing, the hesychasts. . . believed that they attained a vision of divine light and so union with God.

John Meyendorff explains the real purpose of prayer to the hesychast: *The Jesus prayer is at the center of all hesychast spirituality. The Name of the Incarnate Word is bound up in the essential functions of being: it is present in the "heart," it is linked to the breath. . . .The monk is called to become conscious of the actual presence of Jesus in the interior of his own being. . . without any images.*

The knowledge of God within was the goal of *hesychia*, and this was to be achieved without the use of images, thus the widespread iconoclasm of the Orthodox Church. The only art images inherited by us from the Byzantine Christian period are the icons depicting hauntingly beautiful faces of the Virgin or of saints, portrayed not in realistic and natural terms, but rather as symbolic of mystical experience. When one looks at a Russian icon of a saint, for instance, one never knows what the saint *looked like*, but one knows him *mystically*, as though the art of icons had been developed to transport the viewer to another realm, to the kingdom of God, and was never intended to portray things and people of this world.

By the sixth century, the various strands of early desert hesychasm were drawn together in a theological synthesis of its Neoplatonic and biblical

*Black Madonna, gilded wood, 17th century. Notre-Dame-aux-Neiges, Aurillac, France.*

elements. The Hellenistic influence, coming through Neoplatonic thinkers such as Evagrius Ponticus, emphasized "mental prayer" and tended toward a Platonic dualism of body and spirit. The biblical approach, epitomized by Saint Macarius, a contemporary of Athanasius, was instead heart-centered and holistic. Macarius regarded sin as a force that breaks up the unity of the person understood as a single organism. Drawing from the holistic image of the Christ physically incarnate, Macarius emphasized the participation of the whole person in prayer—the body, mind, imagination, soul, and feelings, all compositely represented as "the heart":

*Christ came to reestablish the unity of the human composite; and by constantly recalling the name of Jesus the hesychast makes the grace of redemption live within him. That this grace may be truly efficacious, he must make "his spirit return into his heart," the center of the psycho-physical organism, and thus reconstitute the original harmony between the parts of the organism.*

The prayer of the heart, as *hesychia* came to be called, is a meditation in five parts:

- Entering a state of quiet without reading, thinking, reasoning, or imagining
- Repeating the Jesus prayer with faith and love and absolute concentration
- Regulating the breathing so it becomes rhythmical and at the same time fixing one's gaze on the heart, the stomach, or the navel, allowing the mind to sink back into the heart—aligning mental, spiritual, and physical energies into the contemplation of Oneness
- Feeling inner warmth arising that may develop into the sensation that a fire is burning inside the heart
- Attaining deification, or *theosis*, the state of God-within, through absolute contemplation. The goal of *hesychia* is to unite one's heart with the heart of God, so that the quality of God-consciousness begins to arise in the individual who is practicing this meditation

The heart-centered spirituality of hesychasm—reaching God through the totality of being—was systematized in the sixth century by Saint John Climacus of Sinai. Striking a theme that became crucial in later theological developments, Climacus and his contemporaries did not pose a contrast between the body and the mind or spirit, as developed later in the West. The Eastern Church Fathers did not privilege any aspect of the human organism as being closer to the divine vision than any other. Instead, they depicted all elements of the human person as equally "fallen" in the face of God's utter transcendence, and thereby all parts—body, mind, imagination, and soul (compositely represented as "the heart")—as

The eastern christian tradition thrives today as the Russian Orthodox Church.

equally benefiting from the gifts of grace conferred upon the believer practicing hesychia. The contemporary Greek mystic and psychologist Hierotheos Vlachos summarizes the teachings of the Church Fathers in this respect:

> Saint Gregory the Theologian regarded hesychasm as essential for attaining communion with God. "It is necessary to be still in order to have clear converse with God and gradually bring the mind back from its wanderings." With stillness a man purifies his sense and his heart. So he knows God, and this knowledge of God is his salvation.

Hesychasm flourished, and continues to flourish, in the desert monasteries and at the holy mountain in northern Greece, where monks from many parts of the world spend a life of prayer and fasting.

View of
St. Georges
Monastery,
Wadi el-Kelt,
Israel. The
monastery was
named after the
Holy St.
George of
Koziba, and
was founded in
480 C.E.

*The Russian Pilgrim*

There is a beautiful Russian story that illustrates the power of *hesychia* to cause a deep religious experience found in the classic little book *The Way of a Pilgrim*:

A pilgrim had heard the injunction in the New Testament to pray without ceasing, and he kept asking what it meant and how it could be put into practice. He then met an old monk who urged him to pronounce the name of Jesus with lips and heart at all times and in all places, even during sleep. The pilgrim was to say, "Lord Jesus Christ, have mercy on me," and the monk assured him that not only would the prayer bring deep consolation, but it would also repeat itself without any effort on his part. The old monk quickly became the pilgrim's *starets*, or spiritual father, gave him a rosary, and told him to recite the prayer three thousand times each day, then six thousand times, then twelve thousand times—whether standing or sitting or lying down. Soon, just like the *starets* had predicted, the pilgrim found that the prayer was reciting itself without any effort on his part. "It was as though my lips and tongue pronounced the words entirely of themselves without any urging from me." Then, alas, the *starets* died. The pilgrim bought a copy of *The Philokalia*, put it in his breast pocket with his Bible, and went on his way, always reciting the name of Jesus.

After a while he was surprised to discover that a new development had taken place. The prayer entered his very body: "It seemed as though my heart . . . began to say the words of the prayer with every beat . . . . I gave up saying the prayer with my lips. I simply listened carefully to what my heart was saying. It seemed as though my eyes looked right down into it."

He felt some pain in his heart and a great love for Jesus. Then there came into his heart "a gracious warmth," which spread through his whole breast. And all the time he kept his relationship with his beloved, departed *starets*, who even appeared to him in a dream, giving him guidance and courage.

In this way the Jesus prayer became his whole life, giving him joy and consolation while alone and filling him with love and compassion for all he met on his way.

The Desert Fathers developed a literary and theological style of writing, the core of which focuses on the intimacy between God and the individual. Their sayings, handed down orally, were collected in the *Verba Seniorum*. Thomas Merton wrote of them, "The Desert Fathers declined to be ruled by men, but had no desire to rule over others themselves. Nor did they fly from human fellowship. The society they sought was one where all men were truly equal, where the only authority under God was the charismatic authority of wisdom, experience, and love." The stories of the Desert Fathers were first collected and translated into Latin in the seventeenth century by Rosweyde in a folio book entitled *Vitae Patrum*, and in its introduction we read about the settings where these mystics lived:

> *The place called Scete is set in a vast desert, a day and a night from the monasteries of Nitria; and it is reached by no path, nor is the track shown by any landmarks of the earth, but one journeys by the signs and courses of the stars. Water is hard to find. . . . Here abide men perfect in holiness.*
>
> *There is another place in the inner desert. . . called Celia. To this spot those who have had their first initiation and who desire to live a remoter life, stripped of all its trappings, withdraw themselves: for the desert is vast, and the cells are sundered from one another by so wide a space, that none is in sight of his neighbor, nor can any voice be heard. One by one they abide in their cells, a mighty silence and a great quiet among them.*

The Desert Fathers were spiritual athletes who submitted themselves to all the rigors of a marathon to reach God. They have left us stories that are strangely similar in character to the anecdotes of Zen Buddhism—perhaps because the cultivation of emptiness in the remoteness of a desert gives rise to a deeper sense of essence.

A brother in Scete happened to commit a fault, and the elders assembled, and sent for Abbot Moses to join them. He, however, did not want to come. The priest sent him a message, saying: "Come, the community of the brethren is waiting for you." So he arose and started off. And taking with him a very old basket full of holes, he filled with it sand, and carried it behind him. The elders came out to meet him. "What is this, Father?" The elder replied: "My sins are running out behind me, and I do not see them, and today I come to judge the sins of another!" They, hearing this, said nothing to the brother but pardoned him.

A brother asked one of the elders, saying: "There are two brothers, of whom one remains praying in his cell, fasting six days at a time and doing a great deal of penance. The other one takes care of the sick. Which one's work is more pleasing to God?" The elder replied: "If that brother who fasts six days at a time were to hang himself up by the nose, he could not equal the one who takes care of the sick."

A certain brother while he was in the community was restless and frequently moved to wrath. And he said within himself, "I shall go and live in some place in solitude: and when I have no one to speak to or to hear, I shall be at peace and this passion of anger will be stilled." So he went forth and lived by himself in a cave. One day he filled a jug for himself with water and set it on the ground, but it happened that it suddenly overturned. He filled it a second time, and again it overturned: and he filled it a third time and set it down, and it overturned again. And in a rage he caught up the jug and broke it. Then when he had come to himself, he thought he had been tricked by the spirit of anger and said, "Behold, here am I alone, and nevertheless he hath conquered me. I shall return to the community for in all places there is need for struggle and for patience and above all for the help of God." And he arose and returned to his place.

*Abbot Lot came to Abbot Joseph and said: "Father, according as I am able, I keep my little rule, and my little fast, my prayer, meditation, and contemplative silence; and according as I am able I strive to cleanse my heart of thoughts; now what more should I do?" The elder rose up in reply and stretched out his hands to heaven, and his fingers became like ten lamps of fire. He said:"Why not be totally changed into fire?"*

*Rising in Grace*

Eastern Christendom appropriated the desert tradition not only by emulating the mystical practices of the early saints but also in theology—even in Church dogma. The desert ideal exalted experience, and it is crucial to remember the role of spiritual experience in generating the original dogmas of the Church. Fritjof Capra and Brother David Steindl-Rast in their book *Belonging to the Cosmos: Explorations on the Frontiers of Science and Spirituality* explain the centrality of the individual experience of God for Eastern Christian mysticism:

*Originally the term theology was applied not to the systematic study of religious dogma but to mystical experience. . . . What is remarkable about early Christian thought is that both the Orthodox Fathers and the "heretics" had basically the same view of theology's purpose: to initiate the believer into a genuine gnosis, an experiential knowledge of God.*

The early twentieth century Russian theologian Vladimir Lossky affirmed that the Eastern tradition has never made a sharp distinction between mysticism and theology when he declared, "There is no Christian mysticism without theology; but, above all, there is no theology without mysticism. . . . Mysticism is the perfecting and crown of all theology: it is theology par excellence."

Jesus of the Gospel is the Word made flesh. In the same way that the body of Jesus is the vessel for the divine, so too is our own body. The East has always firmly believed that the body, through contemplative prayer, can become the recipient of divine grace, attaining greater and greater degrees of light until the soul becomes united with God.

*The Ascent to the Heavenly Paradise*, oil on wood by Hieronymous Bosch, 15th c. Palace of the Doge, Venice.

157

*Gregory of Nyssa (335-394)*

The great mystic Gregory of Nyssa is one of the most powerful and influential of all Christian mystics. He was a philosophical theologian and a leader of the orthodox party in the fourth-century Christian controversies over the doctrine of the Trinity. He was born in Caesarea, a town in Cappadocia, Asia Minor (now Kayseri, Turkey), in 335, the younger son of a distinguished family. Gregory was educated in his native province but was more deeply influenced by his philosophical training than by the other two Cappadocian Fathers of the Church, his brother Basil of Caesarea and their friend Gregory of Nazianzus. In the 360s he turned to religious studies and Christian devotion, perhaps even to the monastic life, under Basil's inspiration and guidance. As part of Basil's struggle with Bishop Anthimus of Tyana—whose city became the metropolis (civil and therefore ecclesiastical capital) of western Cappadocia in 372—Gregory was consecrated as bishop of Nyssa, a small city in the new province of Cappadocia Secunda, which Basil wished to retain in his ecclesiastical jurisdiction. In 375, however, Gregory was accused of bad administration by the provincial governor as part of the Arianizing campaign of the Roman emperor Valens (an attempt to force the Church to accept the views of the heretic Arius, who denied the divinity of Christ). He was deposed in 376 by a synod of bishops and banished. But on Valens's death in 378 his congregation welcomed him back enthusiastically. In 381 he took part in the General (second ecumenical) Council at Constantinople and was recognized by the emperor Theodosius as one of the leaders of the orthodox communion in Cappadocia.

Platonic and Christian inspiration combine in Gregory's ascetic and mystical writings, which have been influential in the devotional traditions of the Eastern Orthodox Church and (indirectly) the Western Church. *On Virginity* and other treatises he wrote on the ascetic life are crowned by the mystical *Life of Moses*, which treats the thirteenth-century-B.C.E. journey of the Hebrews from Egypt to Mount Sinai as a pattern of the progress of the soul through the temptations of the world to a vision of God. A notable emphasis of Gregory's teaching is the principle that the spiritual life is not one of static perfection but of constant progress. He saw the spiritual path as a progressive rising in grace. In the following passage Gregory explains the parable quoted in Matthew's gospel as a symbol of the soul rising in grace:

The pure of heart will see God, *according to the Lord's infallible word (Matthew 5:8), according to his capacity, receiving as much as his mind can sustain; yet the infinite and incomprehensible nature of the Godhead remains beyond all understanding.* For the magnificence of his glory, *as the prophet says, has no end, and as we contemplate Him He remains ever the same, at the same distance above us. The great David enjoyed in his heart those glorious elevations as he progressed from strength to strength; and yet he cried to God:* Lord, thou art the most high, forever and ever. *And by this I think he means that in all the infinite eternity of centuries, the man who runs toward Thee constantly becomes greater as he rises higher, ever growing in proportion to his increase in grace.* Thou, indeed, art the most High, *abiding forever, and canst never seem smaller to those who approach Thee for Thou art always to the same degree higher and loftier than the faculties of those who are rising.*

*This, then, is the doctrine the Apostle is teaching about the ineffable nature of the Good, when he says that the eye does not know it even though it may see it. For the eye does not see it completely as it is, but only insofar as it can receive it. So too, even though we may constantly listen to the Word, we do not hear it completely according to its manifestation. And even though the clean of heart use his eyes as much as he can, yet it has not entered into the heart of man. Thus though the new grace we may obtain is greater than what we had before, it does not put a limit on our final goal; rather, for those who are rising in perfection, the limit of the good that is attained becomes the beginning of the discovery of higher goods. Thus they never stop rising, moving from one new beginning to the next, and the beginning of ever greater graces is never limited of itself. For the desire of those who thus rise never rests in what they can already understand; but by an ever greater and greater desire, the soul keeps rising constantly to another which lies ahead, and thus it makes its way through ever higher regions towards the transcendent.*

## Pseudo-Macarius (c. fourth century)

Pseudo-Macarius is the mysterious author of a set of fifty spiritual homilies that focus on the total and existential encounter with God in the heart. The manuscripts were written in the second half of the fourth century and are attributed to several different authors who could have adopted the nom de plume Macarius in compiling the homilies. Saint Macarius the Egyptian has been identified as one of the possible authors: he entered the desert of Scetis when he was thirty years old and lived as a hermit for sixty years, becoming renowned for his great gifts of spiritual direction of hermits and for his healing and prophetic powers. Other possible authors include a Siryan monk, a monk from Mesopotamia, and a citizen of the Roman Empire. Because the true identity of the author cannot be established, the term Pseudo-Macarius is now used instead.

Pseudo-Macarius writes that God is found in a holistic manner within the heart and not in the mind. He insists on the total encountering in ever increasing awareness and even on feeling the presence of the divine. In his homilies he writes of the heart as the place where God meets man in concrete existence. The divinizing effect of the Holy Spirit works through grace into ever mounting levels of transcendence. This spirituality integrates body, mind, and spirit, and prayer is the method by which man experiences God's presence in the purified Christian heart.

> *Know, O man, your nobility and dignity. How precious you are, the brother of Christ, the friend of the King, the bride of the heavenly Bridegroom. For he who is capable of knowing the dignity of the soul is able to know the power and the mysteries of the Godhead and thereby is capable of being all the more humbled, since in the light of God's power does a person see his fallen state.*

Die Heilung des
Gichtbruchigen,
illumination
from the
Goldenes
Evangelienbuch
Heinrich III,
c. 1050.

*The Christian religion is not an ordinary thing. "This mystery is great"*
*(Eph 5:32). Acknowledge your nobility, that you are chosen to a kingly*
*dignity, "a chosen race, a royal priesthood and a holy nation." For the mys-*
*tery of Christianity is foreign to this world. The visible glory of the king and*
*his wealth are earthly and perishable and pass away. But that kingdom and*
*riches are divine things, heavenly and full of glory, never to pass away or*
*to be solved.*

*Christianity is similar to tasting deeply of truth, eating and drinking of*
*truth—to eat and drink on and on to power and energy. It is like a certain*
*spring when someone very thirsty begins to drink from it. But then, while he*
*is drinking, someone rushes him off before he has drunk his full. Afterward,*
*he burns more ardently, because he has tasted the water and eagerly seeks it.*
*So also in the spiritual life, a person tastes and partakes of the heavenly food,*
*but while he is eating it is taken away and no one gives him to eat his full.*

*Dionysius the Areopagite (500-?)*

Probably one of the most enigmatic figures of Eastern Christendom, Dyonisius the Areopagite was a Syrian monk born in the year 500 who, known only by his pseudonym, wrote a series of Greek treatises and letters for the purpose of uniting Neoplatonic philosophy with Christian theology and mystical experience. His writings established a definite Neoplatonic trend in a large segment of medieval Christian doctrine and spirituality—especially in the Western Latin Church—that has determined facets of its religious and devotional character to the present time.

His writings consisted of treatises—*On the Divine Names, On Mystical Theology, On the Celestial Hierarchy,* and *On the Ecclesiastical Hierarchy*—that form a complete theology, covering the Trinity and angelic world, the incarnation and redemption, and provides a symbolic and mystical explanation of all that is. The system designed by Dionysius revolved around "crisis theology—from the Greek word *crisis* meaning "crossroads, decision," by which mystical experience is the simultaneous affirmation and denial of paradox in any statement or concept relative to God. Consequently the incarnation of the Word, or Son of God, in Christ was the expression in the universe of the inexpressible, whereby the One enters into the world of multiplicity. Dyonisius believed that whatever names we give to God are limited forms of communicating the incommunicable. In *Divine Names* and *Mystical Theology* he treats the nature and effects of contemplative prayer, *hesychia,* and the disciplined abandonment of senses and intelligible forms to prepare for the immediate experience of "light from the divine darkness."

The Western mystic Thomas Aquinas wrote commentaries on the writings of Dionysius the Areopagite. The fourteenth- and fifteenth-century Rhineland and Flemish mystics such as Meister Eckhart and Mechtild of Magdeburg, and the sixteenth-century Spanish mystics all were influenced by Dionysian thought.

162

*Trinity!! Higher than thy being,*
*any divinity, any goodness!*
*Guide of Christians*
*in the wisdom of heaven!*
*Lead us up beyond unknowing and light,*
*up to the farthest, highest peak*
*of mystic scripture,*
*where the mysteries of God's Word*
*lie simple, absolute and unchangeable*
*in the brilliant darkness of a hidden silence.*
*Amid the deepest shadow*
*they pour overwhelming light*
*on what is most manifest.*
*Amid the wholly unsensed and unseen*
*they completely fill our sightless minds*
*with treasures beyond all beauty.*

*Leave the senses and the workings of the intellect, and all that the sense and the intellect can perceive, and all that is not and that is; and through unknowing reach out, so far as this is possible, toward oneness with him who is beyond all being and knowledge. In this way, through an uncompromising, absolute and pure detachment from yourself and from all things, transcending all things and released from all, you will be lead upwards toward that radiance of the divine darkness which is beyond all being.*

*Entering the darkness that surpasses understanding, we shall find ourselves brought, not just out of speech, but to perfect silence and unknowing.*

*Emptied of all knowledge, man is joined in the highest part of himself, not with any created thing, nor with himself, nor with another, but with the One who is altogether unknowable; and in knowing nothing, he knows in a manner that surpasses understanding.*

*Gottesmutter
Iverskaja,*
Russian icon,
19th century.
Private
collection,
Frankfurt.

*Theophan the Recluse (1815-1894)*

> *Those who love blessed solitude lead a life of activity that reflects their spiritual powers. They never weary of praising their Maker to all eternity— so that he who ascends to the heaven of solitude never ceases to praise his Creator.*

Theophan the Recluse, perhaps one of the greatest mystics of Eastern Christendom, lived as a recluse-hermit in the monastery of Vysha in Russia until he died at the age of 79 in 1894. During his lifetime he translated from the Greek *The Philokalia* as well as many letters detailing spiritual direction. Apart from these works, the majority of his own writings have yet to become accessible to Western audiences since they have not been translated, even though he is deemed the greatest Russian writer on mystical subjects.

Theophan died in Russia in the nineteenth century, but he retained a real sense of the Christianity of those early Fathers of the third and fourth centuries, a mystical tradition now mostly lost to us: his was a Christian Science of changing men. He was a bishop who withdrew from life to become a *staretz*—a term used in the Russian Church to describe an enlightened teacher.

Theophan was the son of a priest and lived steeped in an atmosphere of Orthodox Christianity from his youth. He went to Kiev Theological Academy, where in 1841 at the age of twenty-six he became a master of theology and a hieromonk. He then undertook a seven-year journey to Jerusalem, and in 1859 he became bishop of Tambov, making a powerful impression on his congregation. In 1863 he became bishop of Vladimir, only to resign three years later when he entered the monastery of Vysha to become an anchorite, and after six years of monastic life he withdrew completely into his cell. There he wrote two major texts on mysticism, *The Path of Salvation* and *What the Spiritual Life Is and How to Attune Oneself to It*. He died in his cell, and in 1988 he was canonized as part of the celebrations for the millennium of the Russian Orthodox Church.

*On Prayer*

*Why hurry in prayer? We spend hours in other pursuits without noticing the passage of time, yet we no sooner stand up to pray that we wonder how long we have been standing. Then we drive ourselves to finish quickly, so it is all profitless.*

*What is the best way to deal with this? Some people pledge themselves to a quarter of an hour of prayer, or half an hour, or an hour as it suits them, then they go on standing at prayer until their time is up by the clock. . . . It is no use hurrying the reading of prayers. . . .*

*Prayer is a spiritual barometer for self-observation. Just as a barometer shows us how heavy or light the air is, so prayer shows us how high or low our spirit has gone in its relationship to God.*

*[A] truly spiritual life is not possible without prayer—which is spiritual life in action. Prayer is the raising of our mind and heart to God. One may say that to pray means bringing right feelings and attitudes into actions.*

*On Magnetization Towards God*

*The aim is to strive towards God; but at first this is done only in intention. It must be made into our actual life—a natural gravitation that is sweet, voluntary and permanent. This is the kind of attitude that shows us when we are on the right track; that God accepts us and that we are moving towards Him. When iron clings to a magnet it is because the power of the magnet draws it. In spiritual matters the same thing is true; it is only clear that God is touching us when we experience this living aspiration; when our spirit turns its back on everything else and is fixed on Him and carried away.*

*At first this will not happen; the zealous person is still turned wholly to himself. Even though he has "decided" for God, this is only in his mind. The*

*Lord does not yet let Himself be tasted, nor is the man yet capable of it, being impure. Then as his heart begins to be purified and set right, he begins to feel the sweetness of a life pleasing to God, so that he begins to walk in His ways gladly and with love. It becomes his natural element, in which he delights. Then the soul starts to withdraw from everything else as from the cold, and to gravitate towards God, Who warms it.*

*This principle of gravitation is implanted in the fervent soul by divine grace. By its inspiration and guidance the attraction grows in natural progression, inwardly nourished even without the knowledge of the person concerned. The sign of this birth is that where the spirit in someone previously acted compulsively, it now begins to abide in God's presence willingly and quietly without strain, with feelings of reverence, fear and joy. Once the spirit was cramped within him, but now it is settled and stays there permanently. Now it is bliss for him to be alone with God, away from others and oblivious to external things. He acquires the Kingdom of God within himself, which is peace and joy in the Holy Spirit. This immersion in God is called "silence of the mind" or "rapture in God."*

The spirit of Eastern mystics burned with spiritual fire. If one could describe the difference between the brothers and sisters of the Eastern and Western mystical traditions, one would perhaps draw from the natural elements of fire and water. The Eastern way is to set the individual aflame, burning all debris accumulated by ego, personality, and knowledge until one becomes pure essence, a pure flame that grows higher and higher until it joins God. The Western way is fluid, flowing; mystics like Hildegard of Bingen or Meister Eckhart sing songs of mystical transport that flow through the centuries and touch us today; the Western way is like an ocean that spreads far and wide to embrace the whole cosmos and drowns Godliness in every drop of water.

# PART III

## SEEKING THE TRUTH

# Chapter Six

## Meditation and Prayer

*May we presume that everyone knows what prayer is? From one point of view the answer is "yes." Every human being knows prayer from experience. Have we not all experienced moments in which our thirsting heart found itself with surprise drinking at a fountain of meaning? Much of our life may be a wandering in desert lands, but we do find springs of water. If what is called "God" means in the language of experience the ultimate source of Meaning, then those moments that quench the thirst of the heart are moments of prayer. They are moments when we communicate with God, and that is, after all, the essence of prayer.*

Holy Mary, Exeter Cathedral.

But do we recognize these meaningful moments as prayer? Here, the answer is often "no." And under this aspect we cannot presume that everyone knows what prayer is. It happens that people who are in the habit of saying prayers at certain set times have their moments of genuine prayer precisely at times when they are not saying prayers. In fact, they may not even recognize their most prayerful moments as prayer. Others who never say formal prayers are nourished by moments of deep prayerfulness. Yet, they would be surprised to learn that they are praying at all. . . . Sooner or later we discover that prayers are not always prayer. That is a pity. But the other half of that insight is that prayer often happens without any prayers. And that should cheer us up. In fact, it is absolutely necessary to distinguish between prayer and prayers. At least if we want to do what Scripture tells us to do and "pray continually" (Luke 18:1) we must distinguish praying from saying prayers. Otherwise to pray continually would mean saying prayers uninterruptedly day and night. We need hardly attempt this to know that it would not get us very far. If, on the other hand, prayer is simply communication with God, it can go on continually. In peak moments of awareness this communication will be more intense, of course. At other times it will be low key. But there is no reason why we should not be able to communicate with God in and through everything we do or suffer and so "pray without ceasing" (1 Thess. 5:17).

But even for us, it is never too late to recover that prayerfulness which is as natural to us as breathing. The child within us stays alive. And the child within us never loses the talent to look with the eyes of the heart, to combine concentration with wonderment, and so to pray without ceasing. The more we allow the child within us to come into its own, the more we become mature in our prayer life. This is surely one meaning of the saying "become like children." There is no childishness suggested here. Jesus says to become not remain like children. We are not to be trapped by the child within us. But neither are we to be alienated from it. A truly mature person has not rejected childlikeness, but rather achieved it on a higher level. As we progress in that direction, everything in our daily life becomes prayer. The childlike heart divines springs of refreshing water at every turn.

—Brother David Steindl-Rast, *Gratefulness, the Heart of Prayer*

ET US IMAGINE FOR A MOMENT THAT WE *KNEW*, absolutely and profoundly, that everything we are and everything we do is prayer; that as an emotion arises within us it touches the heart of God, as we begin to make a gesture it touches the fabric of God, as a thought emerges in our consciousness it meets with a thought from God. If that were so, we would not only feel bathed in grace, but we would also take full responsibility for everything we do and everything we are. If God is listening to our prayers and granting them as they arise, then we should pay full attention to what we ask. If everything is prayer and every prayer is answered, then each one of us is capable of transforming the quality of life for the entire planet. And it is because we don't know that everything is prayer and that our prayers are answered, that we perpetuate destructive cycles in our own lives and in the lives of others, since we think, somehow, that everything we do will have no consequence, and we do not have to take responsibility for our actions, thoughts, and feelings. If this were a God-woven universe in which both human and divine dimensions intermingled, then we would become the guardians of this sacred universe and our actions would be prayerful, because we would want to express profound gratitude for the inheritance of the divine part of ourselves.

This may be a dream of a symphony orchestrated by God with humanity as its instruments, but it is also a metaphor that could help us in the realization that there is a point of contact between each one of us and God, and when contact is made prayer is the spark. Prayer is the sense of contact, as Brother David Steindl-Rast explains in the passage quoted above, not something we do but rather something we are, an all-pervasive feeling of awe that we become "when our thirsting heart [finds] itself with surprise drinking at a fountain of meaning." What Scripture tells us in the term "unceasing prayer" is that that all-pervasive awe, that point of contact between our heart and the heart of God, is a constant, that the spark of prayer happens every millisecond, in every breath, in every gesture, in every feeling.

How, then, can we recapture that knowledge, return to the awareness of prayer as something we are? Where can we start? The only and best way is to start right from where we are, during an ordinary day and doing ordinary activities. If we remember to bring into what we do the quality of prayer, what we do will become prayerful, injected with beauty, and we will feel peaceful, calm, relaxed, and joyful in doing it. This is grace. And out of gratefulness for that quality, we pray some more, bringing prayerfulness into our next day or next activity. Prayer is the outer expression, and meditation the inner expression, of that spark that happens when we touch God. Both prayers and meditations have been created to give us a structure within which we can feel the spark, but it can also be ignited in simple, ordinary things and activities. Brother Steindl-Rast offers again his insight on

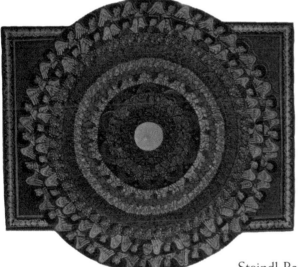

*Hildegard's Sixth Vision: the Choirs of Angels praise the Lord, by Hildegard of Bingen, 12th century.*

how we maintain the quality of prayerfulness—the spark—in even the smallest things, even if we are not being transported by awe:

*Granted, it is not an easy task to maintain the mindfulness, gratefulness, prayerfulness we experience in those wholehearted moments. But at least we know now what we are aiming to maintain. It is like learning to balance a pencil on the tip of a finger. Talking about it is not much help. But when for once we have managed to do it, we know at least that we can do it, and how it is done. The rest is a matter of practice, of doing it over and over again, till it becomes second nature. Applied to prayer, this might mean eating and drinking every mouthful as mindfully as we drink that first cup of coffee. Soon we discover that eating and drinking can be prayer. If we are to "pray without ceasing," how could we stop praying while we eat and drink?*

173

What matters is the inner posture, an inner attitude of meditation, that leads us to unceasing prayer, rather than the content, words, or times of saying prayers. As prayer is the expression of inner meditation, prayer makes us more prayerful. If we remember to alter the focus of our attention from anxiety to meditation a few times a day, then these sacred moments will become like the foundation bricks that build our temple of prayer, and the more we lay at the foundation, the stronger we grow as individuals.

Once we have tasted the quality of prayer in our everyday lives and we see what a huge difference it brings to us—returning us quickly to wholeness and peace—then we need to ask ourselves two basic questions: Are my prayers a genuine expression of my prayerfulness? Do they make me more prayerful? These two questions lead to the matter of focus: is what I do and how I do it a genuine expression of the spark I feel when I am prayerful? And does what I do and how I do it build on the foundation of my feeling prayerful, making me want to deepen that quality in my life? Focus in prayer is like the building of the sacred temple.

This is an inquiry that entails experimentation with different methods, just as we try different foods to find the diet that makes us most healthy, energetic, and joyful. As with diet, prayer demands a degree of constancy; if we were to switch diets every day we would very quickly feel far from healthy. In order to find out if something works for us, we need to try it for a while until we begin to notice the results. So too with prayer. The methods given below are essentially meditations whose focus is prayer. By following one or more of these methods every day for at least three weeks, we will notice a series of progressive stages:

❦ We become accustomed to finding time alone to experiment with deepening our prayerfulness.

❦ We enter the time alone as we would enter through a door—a door into ourselves.

❦ The outer form of the prayer is a way into the realm that exists within us where prayerfulness arises.

❦ As we pray, we explore the feeling of prayerfulness more deeply every day.

❧ The feeling of prayerfulness becomes second nature so that the outer form is no longer the focus of our attention; when this switch occurs, we move from form to essence.

❧ As we learn to move from form to essence, we can experience this movement in our daily activities, always transiting from periphery to content.

❧ The prayer becomes internalized;
we are prayerful.

❧ We bring prayerfulness into other areas of our lives—work, relationships, problems both external and internal.

❧ Our prayerfulness deepens and widens the more prayerful we are.

❧ We become prayer.

❧ We share our prayer with others—our marriages, communities, and temples are enriched.

These stages can be tracked for all the prayers given below as long as you exercise some discipline and take some time off every day when you can be alone and experiment with your prayerfulness. Brother David Steindl-Rast describes the simplicity of one of his own daily prayers:

*To light a candle by myself is one of my favorite prayers. I am not talking about reading prayers by candlelight. The very act of lighting the candle is prayer. There is the sound of striking the match, the whiff of smoke after blowing it out, the way the flame flares up and then sinks, almost goes out until a drop of melted wax gives it strength to grow to its proper size and to steady itself. All this and the darkness beyond my small circle of light is prayer. I enter into it as one enters a room.*

*Centering Prayer*

Centering Prayer is a method that was developed from *The Cloud of Unknowing*, an anonymous mystical text from the fourteenth century, that prepares us to be in the presence of God, opening the door for the spark to be lit that is the flame of our individual contact with God. Centering Prayer is rooted in God's life within us—by praying in this way we allow God to arise within us, to become manifest in everything we do, and to infuse our whole being. We become vessels for the divine. The theological basis of centering prayer is in the renewal of our intimacy with God. In ordinary life, Christians renew their bond with God in the sacraments, beginning with baptism, by which one new-born baby is accepted into the community of seekers. When the sacrament is given, it opens a receptacle for divine love to flow into the baby. So it is with Centering Prayer: we open a possibility of God flowing into us every time we sit for our time of intimacy with Him.

Thomas Keating is a Cisterian monk and former abbot of Saint Joseph's Abbey in Spencer, Massachusetts, and is the founder of the Centering Prayer movement, and these are his instructions for our daily sitting in contemplative prayer:

Guidelines for Centering Prayer

1. Choose a sacred word as the symbol of your intention to consent to God's presence and action within.

2. Sitting comfortably and with eyes closed, settle briefly and silently, introducing the sacred word as the symbol of your consent to God's presence and action within.

3. When you become aware of thoughts, return ever so gently to the sacred word.

4. At the end of the prayer period, remain in silence for a couple of minutes.

*Lectio Divina*

Lectio Divina is a method of contemplative prayer that evolved in monastic enclosures during the Middle Ages. The Christian monastic community is essentially a scriptural environment—the monastery being the place where one is constantly immersed in the Scriptures: at the office, in solitude, in moments of silence, and in a community of similarly minded people.

Medieval monks saw four different levels of depth in Scripture—the literal, the moral, the allegorical, and the unitive. Any passage of Scripture can be read according to these four levels, finding progressively more profound meanings in the same words. This teaching presupposes that Scripture contains a mysterious dynamic that moves one to ever deeper levels of understanding the Word of God. Lectio Divina is also a powerful meditation that can be done every day—as we dwell in the deeper layers of Scripture, so a deeper level of contact between us and God unfolds over the weeks during which this meditation is Practiced.

*The Holy Catherine of Sienna*, painting by Giovanni Battista Tiepolo, c. 1746. Kunsthistorisches Museum, Vienna.

*Lectio Divina Meditation*

Choose a passage from Scripture that you particularly love or that strikes you as containing a powerful meaning. If you are not familiar with Scripture, close your eyes and open a Bible at any point; where your finger rests you will find the passage that you need for this meditation. Read the passage every day for a week, and each time go through the four following steps:

1. Read the passage in its *literal* sense—it will tell you about the historical message and example of Jesus. Think of those biblical times and of life in Jerusalem and of the relationships among the people in the gospel and the Messiah.

2. Read the passage in its *moral* sense—what does the message mean to you? Consider how you can put it into practice in your everyday life. Is there a teaching that can help you in solving a current problem?

3. Read the passage again in its *allegorical* sense—when we realize that the words of Scripture can be applied to our own lives, we

reach a deeper level of understanding: the gospels are about us, the same experience that the disciples and the people in the passage were having with God is the experience we are having right now, during this meditation.

4. Now read the passage in its *unitive* sense—when there is no difference between the feelings evoked by that passage and what you are feeling now. It is as though you yourself had composed the passage and were explaining an experience of God to others. Notice how it feels when one is totally immersed in the word of God and no longer able to distinguish between oneself and Jesus.

There is a spiral movement in the engagement of Lectio Divina. As you return to the same passage every day and read it in its four senses, it gradually begins to take on newer and more and more profound meaning. As you plunge deeper into the meaning of the passage, so your understanding grows, and every day you start where you finished the day before. This spiral movement can also be applied to everyday life; if you are pondering a problem you find difficult to solve, you can write it down and apply Lectio Divina to it, finding deeper levels of meaning every day until a solution will shine forth.

*The Rosary Prayer*

The rosary was created in the Middle Ages, when mass was given in Latin and common folk could not understand all its content. The printing press had not yet been invented, and all manuscripts containing Scripture were kept in monasteries and written in Latin, the language of the learned. The rosary, a string of beads, was a simple yet effective tool by which prayers could be memorized and repeated. Traditionally, a Paternoster (Our Father) was recited on the big bead, followed by ten Aves (Hail Mary) on the ten smaller beads. Each of these groupings—one Paternoster, ten Aves, and a concluding doxology—was known as a decade.

A second method of praying with the rosary was developed, adding to the simple recitation of the vocal prayers a reflection on each of the great mysteries of the faith. Each of the rosary's fifteen decades became associated with one of the great feasts of Jesus and Mary celebrated in the liturgy, such as the Annunciation, the Visitation, the Nativity, the Presentation, and so on. The rosary thus became a true compendium of the liturgy, and those reciting the fifteen decades of the rosary in the course of a day or week were able to access whole areas of Scripture that would otherwise have been closed to them because of lack of education or a knowledge of Latin.

Today we can apply the rosary prayer to our own modern times and choose one word or a simple prayer that is meaningful to us and recite it once a day for, for instance, five decades as a daily devotion. In praying in this way we rest in silence with God, exploring the dimension of calling the essence to fill the form of our prayer. This is a moment of silence, emptiness, and reflection. Here we are, being with God, and nothing else matters at this moment.

*Interior Weeping*

As we become more prayerful, so too our sensitivity will increase. This will be manifested primarily as an intense awareness of suffering—not only our own, but that of the world. Today there is a movement called Deep Ecology, which professes that becoming spiritually aware also leads to an awareness of suffering. If we withdraw from suffering, if we withdraw from touching the wounds, inside and outside us, we cannot ever hope to heal our ruptured relationship with God. Intimacy with God, oneness, is healing. Where there is suffering we bring awareness, care, and attention. We extend our compassion and love unselfishly, and this makes us more prayerful. This is what builds the temple outside.

The first step, however, is to allow ourselves to feel suffering.

Sit quietly on your own, with eyes closed, in darkness.

Slowly, gently focus your attention on the heart of suffering (maybe recall an event that has caused you hurt or violence or sadness. Think of the unfolding of the event and then, when with your mind you are in the midst of

*Maria Himmelfahrt,* by Sano di Pietro, 15th c. Staatl. Lindenau –Museum, Altenburg.

it, switch from the storytelling to the feelings evoked by that episode. Allow your breathing to become slower and to accompany the depth of your emotions. Allow yourself to hurt, to be in sadness, to be in that violence. Allow yourself to become it. This may take some time because we are used to suppressing suffering. Be gentle with yourself and courageous; enter the heart of suffering. If tears well up, allow yourself to cry externally while you are in pain internally. Don't attempt to rush away from what you are feeling. Stay in it; immerse yourself in it until you notice a change.

The change comes when in the midst of intense pain you feel lightness of being. A relief descends upon you, a knot unravels, and conflict becomes peace. Again, slowly and gently, allow yourself to feel this change fully. You will notice that your being is now bathed in light and a new peace of heart has settled upon you.

Repeat this meditation every day for at least a week, and you will notice that you will have permanently acquired a more compassionate attitude toward suffering.

*Prayers*

Prayer is the language of the heart, the only language God speaks. The prayers below are different expressions of devotion, gratefulness, grace, and awe by mystics, known and unknown, throughout the centuries. With prayer we speak with God; God speaks through us when we are prayerful. The moment we listen with the heart, everything makes sense, our distant relationship with God is renewed and becomes intimate, and courage is reestablished.

Prayer is an expression of wonderment, the awe by which we learn God within.

*Oh, watch the day*
*once again hurry off.*
*And the Sun bathe*
*Itself in the water.*
*The time for us to rest approaches.*
*Oh God, who dwelleth in heavenly light.*
*Who reigns above in Heaven's hall.*
*Be for us our infinite light*
*In the valley of the night.*
*The sand in our hour-glass will soon run out.*
*The day is conquered by the night.*
*The glares of the world are ending,*
*So brief their day, so swift their flight.*
*God, let thy brightness ever shine.*
*Admit us to thy mercy divine.*

*And in that day ye shall ask me nothing. Verily, verily, I say unto you,*
*Whatsoever ye shall ask the Father in my name, he will give it to you.*

*Hitherto have ye asked nothing in my name;*
*ask, and ye shall receive, that your joy may be full.*

—John 16:23-24

## The Psalm of David—XXIV

*The earth is the Lord's and the fullness thereof;*
*The world, and they that dwell therein.*
*For it is He who founded it upon the seas,*
*And established it upon the floods.*
*Who may ascend the mountain of the Lord,*
*And who may stand in His holy place?*
*He that has clean hands and a pure heart,*
*Who sets not his heart upon falsehood,*
*Nor swears deceitfully.*
*He will receive a blessing from the Lord,*
*And help from the God of his deliverance.*
*Such is the generation of them that seek Him, O Jacob,*
*Of them that seek His Presence.*
*Lift up your heads, O gates,*
*And be lifted up, you everlasting doors,*
*that the King of glory may enter.*
*Who is the King of Glory?*
*The Lord strong and mighty,*
*The Lord mighty in battle,*
*Lift up your heads, O gates,*
*Lift them up, you everlasting doors,*
*That the King of glory may enter.*
*Who is the King of glory?*
*The Lord of all creation;*
*He is the King of glory.*

## Christian Thanksgiving

*Almighty God, Father of all mercies, we thine unworthy servants do give thee most humble and hearty thanks for all thy goodness and lov-ing-kindness to us and to all men;*

*We bless thee for our creation, preservation, and all the blessings of this life; but above all for thine inestimable love in the redemption of the world by our Lord Jesus Christ, for the means of grace, and for the hope of glory. And we beseech thee, give us that due sense of all thy mercies, that our hearts may be unfeignedly thankful, and that we shew forth thy praise, not only with our lips, but in our lives; by giving up ourselves to thy service, and by walking before thee in holiness and righteousness all our days; through Jesus Christ our Lord, to whom with thee and the Holy Ghost be all honor and glory, world without end. Amen.*

## Breakfast Grace

*Lord, as now we break the fast*
*We thank you for the night safe passed.*
*Now grant safekeeping on our way,*
*Good cheer and strength and health all day.*

—Thomas Elwood

## Prayer Before Meals

*For what we are about to receive,*
*may the Lord make us truly thankful. Amen.*

*We thank Thee, Lord, for happy hearts,*
*For rain and sunny weather.*
*We thank Thee, Lord, for this our food,*
*And that we are together.* —Emilie Fendall Johnson

## Breakfast Prayer

*Father we thank Thee for the night*
*And for the pleasant morning light*
*For rest and food and loving care,*
*And all that makes the day so fair.*

*Help us to do the things we should*
*To be to others kind and good,*
*In all we do, in all we say,*
*To grow more loving every day.*
—Rebecca J. Weston

## Dominican Grace

*We come to join in the banquet of love. Let it open*
*our hearts and break down the fears that keep us*
*from loving each other.*

## Ethiopian Prayer to the Virgin Mary

*O my Lady, the holy Virgin Mary, thou has been likened to many things,*
*yet there is nothing which compares with thee. Neither heaven can match thee,*
*nor the earth equal as much as the measure of thy womb. For thou didst con-*
*fine the Unconfinable, and carry him whom none has power to sustain.*
    *The cherubim are but thy Son's chariot bearers, and even the*
*seraphim bow down in homage at the throne of thy Firstborn. How sub-*
*lime is the honor of thy royal estate. O holy Virgin, instrument of our*
*strength and power, our grace, deification, joy, and fortune; glory of our*

human race! Thou wast the means whereby the salvation of the world has accomplished, and through whom God was reconciled to the sons of humanity. And it was through thee that created human nature was united and indivisible union with the Divine Being of the Creator.

What an unheard-of thing for the potter to clothe himself in a clay vessel, or the craftsman in a handicraft. What humility beyond words for the Creator to clothe himself in the body of a human creature.

And now I cry unto thy Son, O Virgin, saying:

O thou who hast preferred the humble estate of men to the high rank of angels, do not reject thy servant because of the sins I have committed.

Thou whose desire was to partake of earthly rather than heavenly beings, let me share in the secret of thy flawless Divine Being.

Thou to whom Jacob was more comely than Esau, do not scorn me because of my transgressions. For against thee only I have sinned, and much sin have I heaped upon me.

Thou didst create me pure and righteous, yet of my own will I became unclean, and through the persuasion of the wicked one went astray. Thou didst adorn me with gifts of priceless worth which I cast away in favor of unrighteousness.

Make speed, O Lord, to build me into a fortress for the Holy Spirit, Raise me up lest I crumble into a desolate ruin of sin. Make speed to forgive for forgiveness is with thee.

O Lord thou knowest the balm to heal my wounds, the help to strengthen my weakness, the path to prosper my progress. Thou knowest all that is expedient to fulfill my life, as the potter knows how to contrive his own vessel's perfection. For the work is wrought according to the design and wisdom of its maker.

## Saint Patrick's Prayer

*Christ be with me, Christ before me, Christ behind me,*
*Christ in me, Christ beneath me, Christ above me,*
*Christ on my right, Christ on my left,*
*Christ where I lie, Christ where I sit, Christ where I*
*arise,*
*Christ in the heart of every one who thinks of me,*
*Christ in the mouth of every one who speaks of me,*
*Christ in every eye that sees me,*
*Christ in every ear that hears me.*
*Salvation is of the Lord.*
*Salvation is of the Christ.*
*May your salvation Lord, be ever with us.*

## Saint Anthony of Padua's Prayer

*Lord Jesus, bind us to you and to our neighbor with love.*
*May our hearts not be turned away from you.*
*May our souls not be deceived nor our talents or minds enticed by*
*allurements or error,*
*so that we may never distance ourselves from your love.*
*Thus may we love our neighbor as ourselves with strength, wisdom and*
*gentleness.*
*With your help, you who are blessed throughout all ages.*

## Saint Benedict's Prayer

*O Lord,*
*I place myself in your hands and dedicate myself to you.*

*I pledge myself to do your will in all things—*

*To love the Lord God with all my heart, all my soul, all my strength.*

*Not to kill, not to steal, not to covet, not to bear false witness,*
*        to honor all persons.*

*Not to do to another what I should not want done to myself.*

*Not to seek after pleasures. To love fasting. To relieve the poor.*

*To clothe the naked. To visit the sick. To bury the dead.*

*To help in trouble. To console the sorrowing.*

*To hold myself aloof from worldly ways.*

*To prefer nothing to the love of Christ*

*Not to give way to anger.*

*Not to foster a desire for revenge.*

*Not to entertain deceit in the heart.*

*Not to make a false peace. Not to forsake charity.*

*Not to swear, lest I swear falsely.*

*To speak the truth with heart and tongue*

*Not to return evil for evil.*

*To do no injury, indeed, even to bear patient-*
*        ly any injury done to me.*

*To love my enemies.*

*Not to curse those who curse me but rather to*
*        bless them.*

*To bear persecution for justice's sake.*

*Not to be proud.*

*Not to be given to intoxicating drink.*

*Not to be an overeater.*

*Not to be lazy.*

*Not to be slothful.*

*Not to be a detractor.*

*To put my trust in God.*

To refer the good I see in myself to God.

To refer any evil I see in myself to myself.

To fear the day of judgment.

To be in dread of hell.

To desire eternal life with spiritual longing.

To keep death before my eyes daily.

To keep constant watch over my actions.

To remember that God sees me everywhere.

To call upon Christ for defense against evil
thoughts that arise in my heart.

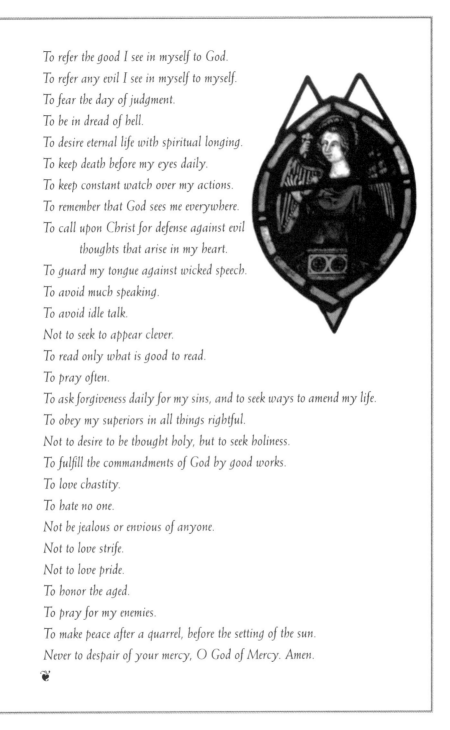

To guard my tongue against wicked speech.

To avoid much speaking.

To avoid idle talk.

Not to seek to appear clever.

To read only what is good to read.

To pray often.

To ask forgiveness daily for my sins, and to seek ways to amend my life.

To obey my superiors in all things rightful.

Not to desire to be thought holy, but to seek holiness.

To fulfill the commandments of God by good works.

To love chastity.

To hate no one.

Not be jealous or envious of anyone.

Not to love strife.

Not to love pride.

To honor the aged.

To pray for my enemies.

To make peace after a quarrel, before the setting of the sun.

Never to despair of your mercy, O God of Mercy. Amen.

*Lord, behold our family here assembled.*

*We thank you for this place in which we dwell,*

*for the love that unites us,*

*for the peace accorded us this day,*

*for the hope with which we expect the morrow;*

*for the health, the work, the food and the bright skies*

*that make our lives delightful;*

*for our friends in all parts of the earth. Amen.*

—Robert Louis Stevenson

## Christian Prayer to Bless the Home

*O eternal God, who alone makest man to be of one mind in a house;*
*Help us, the members of this household, faithfully to fulfill our duties to*
*thee and to each other.*

    *Put far from us all unkind thoughts, anger, and evil speaking.*

    *Give us tender hearts, full of affection and sympathy toward all.*

    *Grant us grace to feel the sorrows and trials of others as our own,*
*and to bear patiently with their imperfections.*

    *Preserve us from selfishness, and grant that, day by day, walking*
*in love, we may grow up into the likeness of thy blessed Son, and be*
*found ready to meet him, and to enter with him into that place which he*
*has gone to prepare for us; for his sake, who liveth and reigneth with thee*
*and the Holy Ghost, one God, world without end.*

*Lord, make us instruments of thy peace.*

*Where there is hatred, let us sow love;*

*Where there is injury, pardon;*

*Where there is discord, union;*

*Where there is doubt, faith;*

*Where there is despair, hope;*

*Where there is darkness, light;*
*Where there is sadness, joy;*
*For thy mercy and for thy truth's sake. Amen.*

—Saint Francis of Assisi

## Dominican Prayer

*May God the Father who made us bless us*
*May God the Son send his healing among us*
*May God the Holy Spirit move within us and give us*
*eyes to see with, ears to hear with and hands*
*that your work might be done.*
*May we walk and preach the word of God to all.*
*May the angel of peace watch over us and lead us at last by God's grace*
        *to the Kingdom.*

*The peace of God, which passeth all understanding, keep your hearts*
*and minds in the knowledge and love of God, and of his Son Jesus*
*Christ our Lord: and the blessing of God Almighty, the Father, the Son,*
*and the Holy Ghost, be amongst you and*
*remain with you always. Amen.*

—Book of Common Prayer

*My prayer is but a cold affair, Lord,*
*because my love burns with so small a flame,*
*but you who are so rich in mercy*
*will not mete out to them your gifts*
*according to the dullness of my zeal,*
*but as your kindness is above all human love*
*so let your eagerness to hear*

be greater than the feeling in my prayers.
Do this for them and with them, Lord,
so that they may speed according to your will
and thus ruled and protected by you,
always and everywhere,
may they come at last to glory and eternal rest,
through you who are living and reigning God through all ages.

—Saint Anselm


Teach us, Good Lord, to serve thee as Thou deservest,
To give and not to count the cost;
To fight, and not to heed the wounds,
To toil, and not to seek for rest;
To labor, and not to ask for any reward,
Save that of knowing that we do Thy will.

—Saint Ignatius Loyola

## Prayer of Saint Bridgid of Ireland


I would like the angels of Heaven to be among us.
I would like an abundance of peace.
I would like full vessels of charity.
I would like rich treasures of mercy.
I would like cheerfulness to preside over all.
I would like Jesus to be present.
I would like the three Marys of illustrious renown to be with us.
I would like the friends of Heaven to be gathered around us from all parts.
I would like myself to be a rent payer to the Lord;
that I should suffer distress, that he would bestow a good blessing upon me.

Around the Throne of God a band
Of glorious Angels ever stand;
Bright things they see, sweet harps they hold,
And on their heads are crowns of gold.

Some wait around Him, ready still
To sing His praise and do His Will;
And some, when He commands them, go
To guard His servants here below.

Lord, give thy Angels every day
Command to guide us on our way,
And bid them every evening keep
Their watch around us while we sleep.

So shall no wicked thing draw near,
To do us harm or cause us fear;
And we shall dwell, when life is past,
With Angels round Thy Throne at last.

—J. M. Neale (1818-66)


We plough the fields, and scatter
The good seed on the land,
But it is fed and water'd
By God's Almighty Hand;
He sends the snow in winter,
The warmth to swell the grain,
The breezes, and the sunshine,
And soft refreshing rain.

All good gifts around us
Are sent from Heav'n above,
Then thank the Lord, O thank the Lord,
For all His love.

He only is the Maker
Of all things near and far;
He paints the wayside flower,
He lights the evening star;
The winds and waves obey Him,
By Him the birds are fed;
Much more to us, His children,
He gives our daily bread.
All good gifts around us
Are sent from Heav'n above,
Then thank the Lord, O thank the Lord,
For all His love.

—Jane M. Campbell

The heavens declare the glory of God; and the firmament sheweth his
        handiwork.
Day unto day uttereth speech, and night unto night sheweth knowledge.
There is no speech nor language, where their voice is not heard.
The line is gone out through all the earth and their words to the end of
        the world. In them hath he set a tabernacle for the sun,
Which is as a bridegroom coming out of his chamber, and rejoiceth as
        a strong man to run a race.
His going forth is from the end of the heaven, and his circuit unto the
        ends of it: and there is nothing hid from the heat thereof.

*The law of the Lord is perfect, converting the soul; the testimony of the*
*Lord is sure, making wise the simple.*

*The statutes of the Lord are right, rejoicing the heart: the commandment*
*of the Lord is pure, enlightening the eyes.*

*The fear of the Lord is clean, enduring for ever: the judgments of the Lord*
*are true and righteous altogether.*

*More to be desired are they than God, yea, than much fine gold:*
*sweeter also than honey and the honeycomb.*

*Moreover by them is thy servant warned: and in keeping of them there*
*is great reward.*

*Who can understand his errors: cleanse thou me from secret faults.*

*Keep back thy servant also from presumptuous sins; let them not have*
*dominion over me: then shall I be upright, and I shall be inno-*
*cent from the great transgression.*

*Let the words of my mouth, and the meditation of my heart, be accept-*
*able in thy sight, O Lord, my strength, and my redeemer.*

—Psalm 19

## Hymn to the Holy Face

*Your picture, Jesus, like a star*
*Is guiding me! Ah, well You know*
*Your Features—grace itself they are—*
*To me, are Heaven here below.*
*Your weeping. . . that, to Love, appears*
*As ornament—attractiveness!*
*I'm smiling while I'm shedding tears*
*At seeing You in your distress.*

To comfort You, I want to be
Unknown, in loneliness. Below
Your Beauty's veiled, and yet to me
Reveals its Mystery! And, oh,
Would I, to you, were flying free!

Your Face. . . my only Homeland, and
The Kingdom, too, where Love has sway:
And it's my smiling meadowland,
The gentle Sun of every day;
The Lily of the Valley—ah,
It's perfume's Mystery! I'm giv'n
What consolation from afar!—
A foretaste of the Peace of Heav'n.

Your Face, that has such tenderness
Is like a sweet reposeful lyre. . .
Bouquet of Myrrh, I would caress
(Such gentleness do You inspire!),
That safely to my heart I'd press. . .

Your Face. . . ah, only that will be
The wealth I ask as revenue:
I'll hide in it, unceasingly;
Then, Jesus, I'll resemble You!
Imprint in me those traits divine
Your Gentleness of Face imparts;
Holiness, then, will soon be mine—
To you I'll be attracting hearts!

*So I can gather souls—it's this,*
*A golden harvest, I desire—*
*Consume me; give me soon, in bliss,*
*That tender burning of Your Fire,*
*Your lips in an eternal Kiss!*
    —Saint Therese of Lisieux


*Dearest Lord, teach me to be generous.*
*Teach me to serve Thee as Thou deservest;*
*To give and not to count the cost;*
*To fight and not to heed the wounds;*
*To toil and not to seek for reward,*
*Save that of knowing that*
*I do Thy will, O God.*
     —Saint Ignatius Loyola


*O Lord my God, shed the light of your love on my*
*child. Keep him safe from all illness and all injury.*
*Enter his tiny soul, and comfort him with your peace*
*and joy. He is too young to speak to me, and to my ears his cries and*
*gurgles are meaningless nonsense. But to your ears they are prayers. His*
*cries are cries your blessing. His gurgles are gurgles of delight at your*
*grace. Let him as a child learn the way of your commandments. As an*
*adult let him live the full span of life, serving your kingdom on earth.*
*And finally in his old age let him die in the sure and certain knowledge*
*of your salvation. I do not ask that he be wealthy, powerful, or famous.*
*Rather I ask that he be poor in spirit, humble in action, and devout in*
*worship. Dear Lord, smile upon him.*
     —Johann Starck

Now that it's over, Lord, thank You, because both my wife and my little boy are doing fine. I've even seen them already, in one of those incubators, fed and wrinkled and, to me, totally beautiful.

You wouldn't think something that small could be alive, but he is, shaking his midget fists at the world and screaming: Look out, I'm here.

He is here, Lord, all here, yet the world won't look out, and he won't have that glass hothouse to protect him like a rose.

He'll have to grow up, and be stepped on, and stand alone against the rain of knocks the world is always too ready to provide. So be with him, Lord, as I will, at least long enough to see his own image made over in the joy of a first child.

—Max Pauli

## Prayer before Study

Grant me, O merciful God, that I might ardently love,
prudently ponder,
rightly acknowledge,
and perfectly fulfill all that is pleasing to you,
for the praise and glory of your Name.

—Saint Thomas Aquinas

## Confessions

Too late I loved you, O Beauty so ancient yet ever new! Too late I loved you! And, behold, you were within me, and I out of myself, and there I searched for you.

—Saint Augustine

## Confessions

*For I remember the kind of man I was, O Lord, and it is a sweet task to confess how you tamed me by pricking my heart with your goad; how you bridged every valley, leveled every mountain and hill of my thoughts; how you cut straight through their windings, paved their rough paths. . .*

—Saint Augustine

## Morning Praise

*To thee, O Master that lovest men, I hasten on rising from sleep; by thy mercy I go forth to do thy work, and I pray to thee: help me at all times, in everything; deliver me from every evil thing of this world and from every attack of the devil; save me and bring me to thine eternal kingdom. For thou art my Creator, the Giver and Provider of everything good; in thee is all my hope, and to thee I ascribe glory, now and ever, and to the ages of ages. Amen.*

—Saint Macarius

*For each new morning with its light,*
*Forest and shelter of the night,*
*For health and food, for love and friends,*
*For everything thy goodness sends.*

—Ralph Waldo Emerson

## Meditations and Devotions

*If Thou sendest evil upon us, it is in love. All the evils of the physical world are intended for the good of Thy creatures, or are the unavoidable attendants on that good. And Thou turnest that evil into good. Thou vis-*

itest men with evil to bring them to repentance, to increase their virtue to gain for them greater good hereafter. Nothing is done in vain, but has its gracious end. Thou dost punish, yet in wrath Thou dost remember mercy.

—John Henry Newman

Be not perplexed,
Be not afraid,
Everything passes,
God does not change.
Patience wins all things.
He who has God lacks nothing;
God alone suffices.

—Teresa of Avila

## Prayer for Joy at Home

Let peace abound in our small company. Purge out of every heart the lurking grudge. Give us grace and strength to forbear and to persevere. Offenders ourselves, give us the grace to accept and to forgive offenders. Forgetful, help us to bear cheerfully the forgetfulness of others. Give us courage and gaiety and the quiet mind.

All shall be Amen and Alleluia.
We shall rest and we shall see,
We shall see and we shall know.
We shall know and we shall love.
We shall love and we shall praise.
Behold our end which is no end.

—Saint Augustine

## The Flowing Light of the Godhead

*Lord, you are my lover,*
*My longing,*
*My flowing stream,*
*My sun,*
*And I am your reflection.*

—Mechtild of Magdeburg

*I am that supreme and fiery force that sends forth all living sparks. Death hath no part in me, yet I bestow death, wherefore I am girt about with wisdom as with wings. I am that living and fiery essence of the divine substance that glows in the beauty of the fields, and in the shining water, and in the burning sun and the moon and the stars, and in the force of the invisible wind, the breath of all living things. I breathe in the green grass and in the flowers, and in the living waters. . . . All these live and do not die because I am in them. . . . I am the Source of the thundered word by which all creatures were made, I permeate all things that they may not die. I am life.*

—Hildegard of Bingen

*Blessed are the poor in spirit: for theirs is the kingdom of heaven.*

*Blessed are they that mourn: for they shall be comforted.*

*Blessed are the meek: for they shall inherit the earth.*

*Blessed are they which do hunger and thirst after righteousness: for they shall be filled.*

*Blessed are the merciful: for they shall obtain mercy.*

*Blessed are the pure in heart: for they shall see God.*

*Blessed are the peacemakers: for they shall be called the children of God.*

—Saint Matthew

## The 23rd Psalm

*The Lord is my shepherd; I shall not want.*

*He maketh me to lie down in green pastures: he leadeth me beside still waters.*

*He restoreth my soul: he leadeth me in the paths of righteousness for his name's sake.*

*Yea, though I walk through the valley of the shadow of death, I will fear no evil: for thou art with me; thy rod and thy staff they comfort me.*

*Thou preparest a table before me in the presence of mine enemies: thou anointest my head with oil, my cup runneth over.*

*Surely goodness and mercy shall follow me all the days of my life: and I will dwell in the house of the Lord for ever.*

## The Lord's Prayer

*Our Father who art in heaven,*
*Hallowed be Thy name,*
*Thy kingdom come,*
*Thy will be done,*
*On earth, as it is in heaven.*
*Give us our daily bread,*
*And forgive us our trespasses,*
*As we forgive them who trespass against us.*
*And lead us not into temptation,*
*But deliver us from evil;*
*For thine is the kingdom,*
*And the power,*
*And the glory,*
*Forever and ever,*
*Amen.*

## Anima Christi

*Soul of Christ, sanctify me,*
*Body of Christ, save me,*
*Blood of Christ, refresh me,*
*Water from the side of Christ, wash me,*
*Passion of Christ, strengthen me,*
*O good Jesus, hear me,*
*Within your wounds hide me,*
*Let me never be separated from you,*
*From the powers of darkness defend me,*
*In the hour of my death call me,*

*And bid me come to you,*
*That with your saints I may praise you*
*For ever and ever. Amen.*

*Holy Spirit, Spirit of the Living God,*
*you breathe in us*
*on all that is inadequate and fragile.*

*You make living water spring even*
*from our hurts themselves.*
*And through you, the valley of tears*
*becomes a place of wellsprings.*
*So, in an inner life*
*with neither beginning nor end,*
*your continual presence*
*makes new freshness break through. Amen.*

—Brother Roger of Taizé

## Psalms 91:14-15

*Because he hath set his love upon me, therefore will I deliver him:*
*I will set him on high, because he hath known my name.*

*He shall call upon me and I will answer him:*
*I will be with him in trouble:*
*I will deliver him, and honor him.*

*Bring us, O Lord God, at our last awak-*
*ening into the house and gate of heaven; to*
*enter into that gate and dwell in that house,*
*where there shall be no darkness nor daz-*
*zling, but one equal light; no noise nor*
*silence, but one equal music, no fears nor*
*hopes, but one equal possession; no ends,*
*nor beginnings, but one equal eternity; in*
*the habitation of thy glory and dominion,*
*world without end. Amen.*

—John Donne

## Evening Prayer

*Lighten our darkness, we beseech thee, O Lord; and by thy great mercy*
*defend us from all perils and dangers of this night.*

## Prayer for Kindling the Lights in Prayers
## for the Pilgrim Festivals

*Almighty God, who art the light of the world, grant us Thy heavenly*
*blessing. May the radiance of these lights, kindled in honor of this*
*Festival, illumine our hearts, and brighten our home with the spirit of*
*faith and love. Let the light of thy Presence guide us, for in Thy light do*
*we see light. Bless also with Thy spirit the homes of all Israel and all*
*humanity, that happiness and peace may ever abide in them. Amen.*

*O Lord, help me to be pure, but not yet.*

—Saint Augustine

*Lord*

*Make me an instrument of your peace.*

*Where there is hatred let me sow love;*

*Where there is injury, pardon;*

*Where there is doubt, faith;*

*Where there is despair, hope;*

*Where there is darkness, light; and*

*Where there is sadness, joy.*

*O divine Master,*

*grant that I may not so much*

*Seek to be consoled as to console;*

*To be understood as to understand;*

*To be loved as to love;*

*For it is in giving that we receive;*

*It is in pardoning that we are pardoned;and*

*It is in dying that we are born to eternal life.*

—Saint Francis of Assisi


*To reach satisfaction in all, desire its possession in nothing.*

*To come to possess all, desire the possession of nothing.*

*To arrive at being all, desire to be nothing.*

*To come to the knowledge of all, desire the knowledge of nothing.*

—Saint John of the Cross

# Epilogue

HERE ARE MANY AND GREAT CHALLENGES that face our spirituality today. If on the one hand we are experiencing an awakening of soul in the world, on the other we must recognize that old ways of accessing spirit are now being ruptured like dams that can no longer contain the river. We live in a post-denominational society in which being a Christian, a Jew, or a Buddhist in the old sense no longer works when we relate as spiritual individuals in search of a common expression of heart. Denominations are like pathways: I choose one path and you another, and we each delve deeply and totally in our religious choices in order to merge with the divine. This was possible in the past, when the world was divided by vast distances of culture, language, social structure, religion, time, and space. Today the world is one, and its very fabric is being torn by deep crises: ecological disaster in this nuclear age and vast overpopulation, with the subsequent problems of unemployment, hunger, disease, and social and political unrest. When so many of the structures that sustain our lives and those of our children are on the brink of dissolution, what we need most urgently is global ecumenism, a coming together in spiritual awakening that unlocks the old denominations and makes us one people working together toward planetary wholeness. What is demanded of us today as spiritual individuals is that we raise our consciousness circles of family, country, race, and religion, that "we love our enemy" and realize that we are all spirits of the earth. Our religion, whatever it may be, needs to celebrate truth on a universal level in order for the way of truth to be reestablished in all world communities.

This vision does not, however, need to deny what being a Christian is and means for each of us individually. At the heart of Christianity exists a long tradition that is creative and that focuses on vision, heart, openness, embracing of suffering, transformation, compassion, acceptance, and community and whose central image is a God in perpetual unfolding to create a global spiritual fire that is kindled by each individual spirituality. This tradition is what Matthew Fox has termed "creation-centered" spirituality, and can be traced back not only to Jesus

himself but to the biblical psalms, the wisdom books of the Bible, and the prophets, and is developed as a theme in many passages of the New Testament. Rather than being something entirely new, this way of Christ is a tradition with historical and biblical roots and supported by saints such as Francis of Assisi and Hildegard of Bingen. It is true that much of Christianity focuses on the Fall from grace and on redemption and toils darkly under a mantle of self-absorption. However, we must not forget that another branch sprung from the same root, one that needs to be revitalized and tended today. The differences between the fall-redemption Christianity and creation-centered Christianity are many, and it is worth listing just a few to unearth the pattern of each:

| *Fall and Redemption Christianity* | *Creation-centered Christianity* |
|---|---|
| Faith is "thinking with assent" | Faith is trust |
| Passion is a curse | Passion is a blessing |
| Mortification of the body | Discipline toward birthing |
| Suffering is wages for sin | Suffering is the birth pangs of the universe |
| Death is wages for sin | Death is a natural event |
| Holiness is the quest for perfection | Holiness is cosmic hospitality |
| Dualistic (either/or) | Dialectical (both/and) |
| Suspicious of the body and violent in its body/soul imagery | Welcoming of the body and gentle in its body/soul imagery |
| Humility is to "despise yourself" (Tanquerry) | Humility is to befriend one's earthiness |
| Pessimistic | Hopeful |
| Elitist | For the many |
| Particular | Universalist |

The creation-centered way of expressing Christian mystical tradition is only in part a departure from traditional values: it is rooted in the past and it is an expression that helps us meet and answer the challenges that modern spirituality faces us with today. We must grow in our wisdom to bring about a religious transformation that will arouse individual responsibility for healing the world. We see suffering around us today in every corner. We must bring freshness, excitement, awe, mystery, and a sense of the spiritual journey back into our Christian expression if we are to accomplish the task at hand; it will take several generations to repair the world and return it to wholeness; therefore we must cultivate spirituality so that it will be a bond and a guide for our children, and their children, and continue down the line of generations. We no longer can work in isolation as holier-than-thou Christians, but we must instead see our path as a global creation, and resuscitate the best sort of mystical expressions, like those of Hildegard or Meister Eckhart, and draw inspiration and strength from them and their vision of Christ as unfolding in this universe.

Start with small steps, and walk a long spiritual path: begin by revitalizing prayer in your life not as a must-do obligation, but as awe and gratefulness. Make your life into a beautiful life, beautify your work, your relationships, and your inner dialogue and catch yourself being prayerful. Perhaps follow one of the courses listed in the section titled The Way of the Heart: A List of Schools and centers

or join a prayer circle. Discuss your choices with your family and friends, awaken their hearts, and let yours be an example to others too. All you are doing is a "yes" to love that will lead inevitably to a deeper understanding of yourself and to a more enlightened future for the world.

—Manuela Dunn Mascetti, September 1997

# The Way of the Heart

Here is a list of schools, centers, and retreat sanctuaries teaching Christian meditation and prayer and other spiritual practices. Several offer retreats and weekly classes. Some focus on group prayer, others offer individual counseling and guidance, and others adopt a more orthodox approach to Christian spirituality and mysticism. Contact the one nearest you and ask for their program and details on how you can enroll. I suggest that you take the plunge and attend one or two classes or prayer practices as soon as possible to get a flavor of meditation and put into practice some of the principles discussed in the book. You will find the staff of all the centers listed here very helpful and welcoming to new students.

## The Christian Heart in Action

Listed here are some organizations whose aim is to make spiritual practice an active program for the community. These centers base their services, including teaching, counseling, outreach programs, and prayer, on extending compassion to the whole human community.

### Silent Unity (Nondenominational)

1901 NW Blue Parkway

Unity Village, MO 64065

Tel: 816/ 246 5400

Toll free: 1-800-669 7729 (within the US only)

For the hearing-impaired—teletypewriter: 816/525 1155

Web site: www.unityworldhq.org

This prayer ministry has been conducting prayer on a continuous basis for over a century—that's nonstop prayer, every day of every week—for more than a hundred years! It began as a small group of friends and is now a worldwide ministry with hundreds of devoted participants who handle requests for help through prayer that arrive at the ministry every day.

Silent Unity conducts a morning prayer meeting every working day to share the *Daily Word* message. At 11 a.m., employees and visitors gather in the chapel for a prayer service. Then there is consecrated prayer at noon and then at 3 and 11 p.m. In addition to these regular gatherings, the workers, one after another, take their turns in the Prayer Vigil Chapel to pray alone every half hour throughout the day. Even at night, the spiritual vigil continues in the small sanctuary. Here in this chapel the prayer requests that are sent in by letter, fax, or telephone are undertaken. Prayer is held for anyone who requests it, whatever denomination, creed or location in the world. Each prayer requested is uttered within the daily vigil for thirty days. There is no counsel given on personal problems but rather a direction towards God through constant prayer.

## Guideposts (Trans-denominational)

16 E. 34<sup>th</sup> Street
New York, NY 10016.
Tel: 212/251 8100
Peale Center: 66 East Main Street, Pawling, NY 12564.
Tel: 914/855 5000
Internet address: http://www.guideposts.org

Guideposts is a family of nonprofit organizations which includes the *Peale Center*, the *Positive Thinking Foundation* and *Guideposts Publications*. Together, these organizations direct their energies and resources to accomplish a vital mission: to be the world leader in communicating positive, faith-filled principles that empower people to reach their maximum personal and spiritual potential.

Guideposts, the brainchild of Dr. Norman Vincent Peale, a minister, and Raymond Thornburg, a Pawling businessman, was founded in March 1945 as a nondenominational forum for people to relate their inspirational stories. The intention was to provide a "spiritual lift" to all readers.

The *Peale Center for Christian Living* in Pawling, New York, offers inspirational publications, audio- and videotapes, seminars, and conferences.

*Guideposts Prayer Fellowship* uses the power of group prayer to help solve problems and make daily living more effective. Prayer Fellowship responds to more than eight thousand requests monthly.

*Dial Guideposts for Inspiration* offers two-minute uplifting messages recorded by Dr. and Mrs. Peale via daily telephone recordings in twenty-seven cities across the United States. More than seven hundred thousand calls are received annually.

*Touchtone for Inspiration* features Dr. and Mrs. Peale as well as Guideposts authors, who have recorded over three hundred inspirational messages relating to twenty-six major categories. The service also offers information about Outreach programs and helpful reprints and booklets.

*Dial-A-Prayer* is a daily message of hope and inspiration followed by a prayer for the day. At the request of the Salvation Army and other organizations, free publications are provided to those affected by natural disasters such as hurricanes and earthquakes.

*The School of Practical Christianity* brings together clergy and their spouses from the United States and abroad in a nondenominational program of personal growth and spiritual renewal.

*The Positive Thinking Foundation* was established in association with Peale Center to develop programs and materials for children of all ethnic and religious backgrounds. The foundation produced the "Positive Kids" video program, which has been widely acclaimed and is available in seven thousand public schools around the country. Designed to help children ages five to nine develop the skills they need to resist negative pressures, the *Positive Kids* program helps them build self-esteem and develop problem-solving techniques.

## Agape, Church of Religious Science

3211 Olympic Blvd.
Santa Monica, CA 90404
Office address: 1904 Centinela Avenue, Santa Monica CA 90404
Tel: 310/829 2780
Tapes of sermons and choir performances—Agape Quiet Mind Bookstore, Tel: 310/829 5780
Prayer Ministry, Tel: 310/453 6638 (24 hours, 7 days)

*Agape International Center of Truth* is the home of the *Agape Church of Religious Science*. It was formed in 1987 to become a trans-denominational church with the world as its community. It was set up in a location where there are many creeds and races and recent interracial tensions, and where such a foundation is a necessary presence. The church, run by the Reverend Michael Beckwith and his staff, has over four thousand active members and twelve thousand friends and twenty ministries and projects dedicated to the realization of the Presence of God, Peace, and Love on this planet, and is a rapidly growing presence on the west coast.

Agape facilitates meditation retreats and Master Practitioner trainings, and the Reverend Beckwith cowrites music for the Agape Choir. Beckwith also hosts a radio ministry titled "Life is Good," which broadcasts every Sunday evening at 8 p.m. Pacific Central time on KYPZ (AM 1230).

Church meetings take place at 8:30 a.m., 9 a.m., 10:30 am., 11 a.m., every day and on Wednesday evenings at 7:15 p.m., with a meditation service at 6:45 p.m.

*The Agape Prayer Ministry* is a part of the Agape International Center of Truth, with a primary focus on prayer. The practitioners engage in prayer as spiritual practice and are available to answer prayer calls twenty-four hours a day, seven days a week. The service is free.

### Glide Memorial Church (Methodist)

330 Ellis Street
San Francisco, CA 94102
Tel: 415/771 6300
Fax: 415/921 6951

Glide Memorial is another unique church based on Methodist belief but encouraging all other faiths to visit. It operates a strong social and environmental presence in San Francisco, including programs for food, computer tutoring, racial problems, and domestic violence prevention training. The services are fabulous: lively, dramatic, filled with gospel singing and dancing. Well worth a visit to experience spiritual transportation while attending mass.

## Retreats and Monasteries

### Dormition of the Mother of God, Monastery for Women (Orthodox Church of America—OCA)

Mother Gabriella, Abbess
3389 Rives Eaton Road
Rives Junction, MI 49277
Tel: 517/569 2873

Founded in 1987, the monastery is located in forty-nine acres of woodland with a cemetery. This is the only monastery in Michigan, and it is a place in which to nurture the spirit of God within. All visitors and guests are invited to attend services and/or send lists of names for intercession. There are ten sisters in residence and two priests.

Private and/or group retreats may be planned for several days. Please call or write for arrangements.

### The Monastery of Christ in the Desert (Benedictine)

Abiquiu, NM 87510
Tel. and Fax: 505/470 5987
Web site: www.christdesert.org

*Christ in the Desert* is located in the beautiful Chama Canyon wilderness in northeastern New Mexico, about 75 miles north of Santa Fe. The minimum stay for guests is two days and two nights, and the maximum stay is two weeks in summer and three weeks in winter. There are five single and four double rooms. Guests are encouraged to participate in the common prayer, share the meals with the monks, and take part in the work schedule of the monastery.

*Gateway Monastery* (Order of Contemplative Monks)
P.O. Box 234
Los Altos, CA 94023
e-mail: rackley@earthlink.net

*The Order of Contemplative Monks* is a community of gay men, living under an adapted Rule of Saint Benedict, who have a desire to dedicate themselves to meditation, prayer, and community service to help others, to give support and counseling to other gay men in crisis or who are in denial or despair, and to help the general community in developing compassion and generosity within their own lives. Meditation and daily prayer in the course of the daily office is supplemented with Gregorian chants and hymns, inspirational readings, individual contemplative study, martial arts, and silence.

*Saint Andrew's Abbey* (Benedictine)
P.O. Box 40
Valyermo, CA 93563
Tel: 805/944 2178 (For retreat information, ask the Guestmaster.)
Fax: 805/944 1076
e-mail: standrab@ptw.com

*Saint Andrew's Abbey* in Valyermo is a Roman Catholic Benedictine monastery of men who have committed themselves to the search of God in corporate prayer, work, and obedience. The basis for monastic life at Valyermo is the Rule of Saint Benedict, a formula for life in community which has been followed by monks and nuns for over fifteen hundred years.

The monks of Saint Andrew's Abbey gather for prayer in the chapel five times a day, where guests are always welcome. Additional time during the morning and evening is spent in *lectio divina*, a slow contemplative reading of the Scriptures which enables the Bible to serve as a means for entering into the presence of God. The monks also engage in a variety of ministries through which the special character of prayer is shared with men and women living in society. The ministry of retreats

213

is conducted at the monastery, where guests of both sexes are welcome to spend time in the Retreat House, sharing in the prayer life of the monks as fully as they wish. Such retreats may be made privately or in groups: accommodation for large groups are available at the Youth Center. The resources of the Monastery Library, a 25,000-volume research library emphasizing patristics and Christian mysticism, can be made available to retreats with genuine research needs. Call the monastery for information on retreats and workshops.

*Holy Cross Monastery*
P.O. Box 99
West Park, NY 12493
Tel: 914/384 6660, ext. 302 for guesthouse
Fax: 914/384 6031
e-mail: guesthouse@idsi.net (for information on retreats)
Web site: www.idsi.net/holycross/guest.html

*Holy Cross Monastery* leads a variety of very interesting seminars and retreats throughout the year, including the *Writers' Workshop, Silent Retreat,* the *Human/Divine Challenge: To Be in Relationship and To Be One's Self, Lenten Retreat, Holy Week and Easter,* the *Benedictine Experience* and many more that are scheduled for 1998. Write to obtain information. Holy Cross Monastery is one of the monastic houses of the Order of the Holy Cross; they are a contemporary Benedictine community of men within the Anglican (Episcopal) community.

*Benedictine Sisters of Mount Saint Scholastica*
Mount Saint Scholastica
801 South 8th Street
Atchinson, KS 66002
Tel: 913/367 6110
Web site: www.benedictine.edu/mount.html

Hospitality is this community's charism. The peaceful setting and the daily communions are conducive to reflection and discernment, learning, discovery, and prayer. Visitors most often comment on the beauty of the campus, and especially on the three chapels, where prayer is ongoing. There are three main ministries. The *Sophia Center* is a Benedictine center for spirituality that is open to persons of all faiths. Its programs address contemporary concerns and empha-

214

size prayer, community, personal integration, and the interconnectedness of creation. This is a peaceful place to get away for private or directed retreats. The *Mount Conservatory of Music* offers artistic training in studio piano, pipe organ, harp, strings voice, woodwinds, brass and handbells. The *Benedictine Volunteer Program* offers an opportunity for men and women to participate in the community life, prayer, and ministry of the sisters.

## The Christian Heart on the Net

These are Internet addresses of Christian communities that offer information on spiritual practice, discussion groups, events, services, retreat centers, and much more.

*SisterSite*: www.sistersite.com
This is an Internet discussion group founded in 1994 and devoted to the history and contemporary concerns of religious women. It provides Internet addresses of women's communities on the Web; information on periodicals, publishers, booksellers, and services of interest to sisters; discussions on history, theology, scripture study and religious studies, women's theology and spirituality, and social justice; and conferences of interest to sisters.

*Contemplative Outreach*: www.io.com/~lefty/AboutCO.html
Centering Prayer was first developed from the ancient practice of contemplative prayer by a group of Trappist monks at Saint Joseph's Abbey in Spencer, MA. Father Thomas Keating resigned as Abbot of Saint Joseph's and moved to Saint Benedict's Monastery in Snowmass, CO, to train teachers in the method. Intensive Centering Prayer retreats are now given at Saint Benedict's Monastery as well as several other locations. In 1984 Contemplative Outreach Ltd. was established to coordinate efforts to introduce the Centering Prayer method to persons seeking a deeper life of prayer and to provide a support system capable of sustaining their commitment. See their Web site for Contemplative Outreach Area and Regional contacts. For Saint Benedict's Monastery and Father Thomas Keating: http://rof.net./wp/theophan/index.html

*Benedictines online*: www.op.org/op
*Franciscans online*: http://listserv.american.edu/catholic/franciscan
*Cistercians online*: www.osb.org/osb/cist
*Dominicans online*: www.op.org/op
*Jesuits online*: http://maple.lemoyne.edu/~bucko/jesuit/html

*Christian Camping International:* cci@cciusa.org
Provides resources for those interested in Christian camping and wilderness activities, including a journal of Christian camping and a directory of more than eight hundred Christian camps throughout the United States.

*Virtual Christianity:* www.ccil.org/%Edwat/spirit.html
Christianity pages from worthy Web resource servers with comprehensive subject listings, including Bibles, Bible studies, apologetics sites, discussions, the *Christian Connection, Christian Internet Directory, Christian Cyberspace Companion,* the *Yankee Christian* and many more.

*Bible Net:* www.biblenet.com
An online source for Christian music, articles, information, and fun.

*Bible Net Library:* www.biblenet.net/library/library.html
Everything on the Bible one could possibly want to know, including archaeology, Scriptures, Bible questions, Bible studies, devotionals, reference materials, and much more.

*A Guide to Christian Literature on the Internet:*
    ftp://iclnet93.iclnet.org/pub/resources/christianbooks.html
A complete reference site on Christian literature. Everything is viewable online—search under categories such as Bibles, Bible Study Aids, Books (listed by title), Collections of Books, etc.

*A Guide to Christian Resources on the Internet:*
    www.iclnet.org/pub/resources/christian-resources.html
Christian indexes and guides, religious study subjects, Web search utilities, Gopher search tools, and everything you need to find Christian resources on the Internet.

*Christian Mysticism Book List:* www.newvision-psychic.com/bookshelf/christian.html
Recommendations and reader reviews of books that explore esoteric and mystical Christianity. Most books are available to be ordered online.

*The Holy Bible*, Revised Standard Version. New York: National Council of the Churches of Christ in the USA, 1957.

*The Holy Bible*, Revised Standard Version. New York: Division of Christian Education of the National Council of the Churches of Christ in the USA, 1946, 1952, 1971.

Archimandrite Cherubim. *Contemporary Ascetics of Mount Athos*. Vol. 1. Platina, CA: Saint Herman of Alaska Brotherhood Press, 1991.

Archimandrite Hierotheos Vlachos. *Orthodox Psychotherapy: The Science of the Fathers*. Levadia, Greece: Theotokos Monastery, 1994.

Barrois, George, trans. and ed. *The Fathers Speak*. Crestwood, NY: Saint Vladimir Seminary Press, 1986.

Capra, Fritjof and David Steindl-Rast. *Belonging to the Cosmos: Explorations on the Frontier of Science and Spirituality*. San Francisco: HarperCollins, 1991.

Climacus, Saint John. *The Ladder of Divine Ascent*. Boston: Holy Transfiguration Monastery, 1991.

French, R. M., trans. *The Way of Pilgrim*. New York: The Seabury Press, 1965.

Fox, Matthew. *The Coming of the Cosmic Christ*. San Francisco: HarperCollins, 1988.

———. *Wrestling with the Prophets*. San Francisco: HarperCollins, 1995.

Guardini, Romano. *The Lord*. Washington, D.C.: Regnery Publishing, 1996.

Harvey, Andrew. *The Essential Mystics*. San Francisco: HarperCollins, 1996.

Jackson Case, Shirley. "The Acceptance of Christianity by the Roman Emperors." In *Papers of the American Society of Church History*. New York: G. P. Putnam's Sons, 1928.

Keating, Thomas. *Intimacy with God*. New York: Crossroad Publishing Company, 1996.

Lang, Paul Henry, *Music in Western Civilization*. New York: Norton, 1994.

Maloney, George A., trans. and ed. *Pseudo-Macarius*. New York: Paulist Press, 1992.

McManners, John, ed. *The Oxford Illustrated History of Christianity*. Oxford: Oxford University Press, 1990.

McNeill, William, *Plagues and Peoples*. Garden City, NY: Doubleday, 1976.

Meyendorff, John. *Saint Gregory Palamas and Orthodox Spirituality*. New York: Saint Vladimir's Press, 1974.

Pelikan, Jaroslav. *The Spirit of Eastern Christendom*. Chicago: University of Chicago Press, 1974.

Shaeffer, Frank. *Dancing Alone: The Quest for Orthodox Faith in an Age of False Religions*. Boston: Holy Cross Press, 1994.

Stark, Rodney. *The Rise of Christianity*. San Francisco: HarperCollins, 1997.

Steindl-Rast, Brother David. *Gratefulness: The Heart of Prayer—An Approach to Life in Fullness*. New York: Paulist Press, 1984.

Waddell, Anne. *The Desert Fathers*. Michigan: University of Michigan Press, 1994.

Ware, Timothy. *The Orthodox Church*. London: Penguin, 1993.

Williams, Esther, trans. *The Heart of Salvation*. Newbury, MA: Praxis Institute Press, 1991.

Wilson, Ian. *Jesus: The Evidence*. San Francisco: HarperCollins, 1996.

FURTHER READING LIST


*The Holy Bible*, Authorized King James Version. New York: Oxford University Press, 1945.

*The Revised English Bible with the Apocrypha*. Oxford and Cambridge: Oxford University Press and Cambridge University Press, 1989.

Amstrong, Edward A. *Saint Francis: Nature Mystic*. University of California Press, 1973.

Blackney, Raymond. *Meister Eckhart: A Modern Translation*. New York: Harper & Row, 1941.

Bloch, Ernst. *Atheism in Christianity*. New York: Herder & Herder, 1972.

Brown, Raymond E. *The Birth of the Messiah:* Garden City, NY: Doubleday, 1977.

Burton-Christie, Douglas. *The Word in the Desert*. Oxford: Oxford University Press, 1993.

Chesterton, G. K. *Saint Thomas Aquinas: The Dumb Ox*. Garden City, NY: Doubleday, 1956.

Clark, *The Great German Mystics*. New York: Russel and Russell, 1949.

Doyle, Brandan. *Meditations with Julian of Norwich*. Santa Fe, NM: Bear & Co., 1983.

Fox, Matthew, ed. *Western Spirituality: Historical Roots, Ecumenical Routes*. Santa Fe, NM: Bear & Co., 1980.

Fox, Matthew. *Breakthrough: Meister Eckhart's Creation Spirituality in New Translation*. Garden City, NY: Doubleday, 1982.

————. *Meditations with Meister Eckhart.* Santa Fe, NM: Bear & Co., 1982.

————. *Original Blessing: A Primer in Creation Spirituality.* Santa Fe, NM: Bear & Co., 1983.

Griffiths, Bede. *Return to the Center.* Springfield, IL: Templegate, 1977.

Haag, Herbert. *Is Original Sin in the Scripture?* Sheed & Ward, 1969.

Harvey, Andrew. *The Return of the Mother.* Berkeley, CA: Frog, 1995.

Lossky, Vladimir. *The Mystical Theology of the Eastern Church.* London: James Clarke & Co., Ltd., 1957.

McDonnell, Ernest W. *The Beguines and Beghards in Medieval Culture.* New Brunswick, N. J.: Rutgers University Press, 1954.

Merton, Thomas. *Conjectures of a Guilty Bystander.* Garden City, NY: Doubleday, 1968.

Miranda, José. *Marx and the Bible.* Orbis Books, 1974.

Moffat, James, ed. *A New Translation of the Bible Containing the New and Old Testaments.* New York: Harper & Row, 1922.

Nolan, Albert. *Jesus Before Christianity.* Orbis Books, 1978.

Pieper, Josef. *Guide to Thomas Aquinas.* New York: Pantheon Books, 1962.

Spidlik, Tomas. *The Spirituality of the Christian East.* Kalamazoo: Cistercian Publications, 1986.

Smith, Huston. *The Illustrated World's Religions.* San Francisco: HarperCollins, 1996.

Tanquerai, Father Adolph. *The Spiritual Life: A Treatise on Ascetic and Mystical Theology.* Westminster, MD: Newman Press, 1930.

Uhlein, Gabrielle. *Meditations with Hildegard of Bingen.* Santa Fe, NM: Bear & Co., 1983.

Westermann, Claus. *Blessing in the Bible and the Life of the Church.* Fortress, 1978.

Wilson, Ian. *Jesus: The Evidence.* San Francisco: HarperCollins, 1996.

Woodruff, Susan. *Meditations with Mechtild of Magdeburg.* Santa Fe, NM: Bear & Co., 1982.

Woods, Richard, ed. *Understanding Mysticism.* Garden City, NY: Doubleday, 1980.

## ACKNOWLEDGMENTS

The following persons were instrumental to the task of preparing, birthing, and finishing the book, and their understanding and support is deeply appreciated: Byron Belitsos for his generosity in opening his library and guiding me through the literature of the Christian East and for allowing me to weave some of the passages from his own essay on Christian Orthodoxy into my own text; my task in completing that part of the book was made much easier with your help. Malcolm, Magda, and Jerome of MoonRunner. Bob Miller, Lisa Jenner Hudson, David Lott of Hyperion. A special thank you also goes to my family: to my parents, and to Stefano, and Flavio for supporting me through the months of writing with good humor and many jokes at the expense of Christian saints! And, finally, an eternal and heartfelt thank you to Philip for always being there, every moment of every day.

Grateful acknowledgment is made for permission to reprint from the following:

Biblical quotes from both the Old and the New Testament in Chapters One and Two from National Council of the Churches of Christ in the USA, Division of Christian Education (New York): *The Revised Standard Version Bible.* Copyright © 1946, 1952, 1971 by the Division of Christian Education of the National Council of the Churches of Christ in the USA, reproduced by kind permission. Subsequent biblical quotes from the New Testament in Chapters One and Two from *The Knox Bible* by Monsignor Ronald A. Knox, copyright © 1944, 1948, 1950 by the Archbishop of Westminster, reproduced by kind permission. Quote by Matthew Fox in Chapter Three from *The Coming of the Cosmic Christ*, copyright © 1988 by Matthew Fox, reproduced by kind permission of HarperCollins, New York. Quote from Rodney Stark in Chapter Three from *The Rise of Christianity*, copyright © 1996 by Rodney Stark, reproduced by kind permission of Princeton University Press, Princeton. Quote in Chapter Four by Matthew Fox from *Wrestling with the Prophets*, copyright © 1995 by Matthew Fox, reproduced by kind permission of HarperCollins, New York. Quoted passages in Chapter Four by Hildegard of Bingen, from *Meditations with Hildegard of Bingen*, edited by Gabrielle Uhlein, copyright © 1983 by Gabrielle Uhlein, reproduced by kind permission of Bear and Co., Santa Fe. Quoted passages in Chapter Four by St. Francis of Assisi, from *The Prayers of St. Francis*, compiled by W. Bader, copyright © 1988 by W. Bader, reproduced by kind permission of Darton, Longman and Todd, London. Quoted passages by Mechtild of Magdeburg in Chapter Four, from *The Revelations of Mechtild of Magdeburg*, translated by Lucy Menzies, copyright © 1953 by Lucy Menzies, reproduced by kind permission of Longmans, Green, London. Last quote by Mechtild of Magdeburg in Chapter Four from *Beguine Spirituality*, copyright © 1989 by Oliver Davies, reproduced by kind permission of Crossroads Publishing, New York. Quoted passages by Meister Eckhart in Chapter Four from *Meditations with Meister Eckhart* with introduction and versions by

Matthew Fox, copyright © 1982 by Matthew Fox, reproduced by kind permission of Bear and Co., Santa Fe. Quoted passages by Julian of Norwich in Chapter Four, from *Julian of Norwich: Showings*, translated by Edmund College and James Walsh, copyright © 1978 by Edmund College and James Walsh, reproduced by kind permission of Paulist Press, New York. Stories of the Desert Fathers in Chapter Five from *The Fathers Speak*, translated and edited by George Barrois, copyright © 1986 by George Barrois, reproduced by kind permission of Saint Vladimir Seminary Press, Crestwood, NY. Stories of the Desert Fathers in Chapter Five from *The Essential Mystics*, edited and introduced by Andrew Harvey, copyright © 1996 by Andrew Harvey, reproduced by kind permission of HarperCollins, New York. Quote by Gregory of Nyssa in Chapter Five from *From Glory to Glory*, copyright © 1979 by Saint Vladimir Seminary Press, Crestwood, NY. Quoted passages by Brother David Steindl-Rast in Chapter Six from *Gratefulness: The Heart of Prayer*, copyright © 1984 by David Steindl-Rast, reproduced by kind permission of Paulist Press, New York. Guidelines for Centering Prayer by Thomas Keating in Chapter Six from *Intimacy with God*, copyright © 1996 by Thomas Keating, reproduced by kind permission of Crossroads Publishing, New York.

## PICTURE ACKNOWLEDGMENTS

*The publishers would like to thank the following for the use of images within this edition.*
**AKG Photo Library**: 5, 12, 17, 21, 27, 28, 33, 41, 44, 57, 60, 72, 75, 84, 89, 96/97, 100, 108, 113, 119, 120, 125, 132, 137, 141, 148, 149, 151, 152, 157, 161, 164, 173, 177, 180; **Ancient Art and Architecture**: 35, 69, 144; **The Bridgeman Art Library**: 24, 36, 105, 129; **ZEFA Pictures**: 85.

The illustration on page 53 and all motifs appearing throughout the book
have been specially created by MoonRunner Design.
Special thanks go to the Dean of Exeter Cathedral, for his kind permission for the photographic
reproduction of many of the stained glass windows and magnificent decorations of the Cathedral.

*Every effort has been made to trace all present copyright holders of the material used in this book, whether organizations or individuals. Any omission is unintentional and we will be pleased to correct any errors in future editions.*